EDITOR'S COMME

This book is a word-for-word copy of Colonel James Smith's original book, "written by himself" and published in 1799. The book was titled:

<u>AN ACCOUNT OF THE REMARKABLE OCCURANCES IN THE LIFE AND TRAVELS OF COL. JAMES SMITH, DURING HIS CAPTIVITY WITH THE INDIANS IN THE YEARS 1755-1759</u>

At the time it was written, the letter *f* was used interchangeably with the letter *s*. This can make for a curious novelty when reading, but also leads to a lot of confusion when trying to understand what a word and passage mean. For example, the word business would be spelled **bufineff**, and likewise all words containing an *s*. However, if a word starts with *s,* the *f* is not used, but all additional *s*'s would be represented by the letter *f*. How confusing that becomes, particularly with words such as sassafras, which would be spelled **saffafraf**!

I trust you will enjoy this remarkable story without its spelling complexities.

I wish to give credit along with my deep appreciation to Suzanne G. Jones, who spent a good part of her wintertime in Florida painstakingly deciphering and typing this manuscript using modern spelling.

Also my loving appreciation to my wife M. Michelle for her encouragement.

And thank you to my daughter Jami Nadzam for her Cover expertise.

Foreword

Colonel James Smith

If you mention Daniel Boone or Davy Crockett, most people would have some familiarity with these important men in our history; but if you mentioned Colonel James Smith, few, if any, would have even the faintest idea of who he was. Yet, James Smith was one of America's outstanding heroes.

Here are a few things of interest about his eventful and amazing life:

He was born in Chester County, Pennsylvania in 1737, captured by the Indians when a teenager, and was adopted into their tribe. He was a prisoner in Fort Duquesne, (Pittsburgh, PA.) during Braddock's Defeat and witnessed the burning of English prisoners. He was adopted into the Caughnawaga tribe and traveled with them throughout the Ohio region, going as far west as the Miami River and Fort Detroit. While with them, he learned their hunting and trapping methods and included them in his book. After five years, he escaped and returned to his home in Pennsylvania. Upon arriving, he found that his sweetheart had given up on his returning to her and had married someone else only a few days prior.

Neil Swanson's 1937 book, The First Rebel, was a biography of Smith and his Black Boys, who he organized to defend their settlement. He taught them the Indian tactics of border warfare, including painting their faces black in the Indian manner for war.

They were the first to take up arms against the British in defense of their Pennsylvania homeland. Shots fired by the Black Boys were nine years prior to the "shot heard 'round the world" at Lexington Green. In 1939, RKO Pictures made a film from Swanson's book starring John Wayne as Jim Smith, called Alleghany Uprising.

Later, Smith crossed the Appalachian Mountains and explored throughout Kentucky and Tennessee, and nearly to the Mississippi River, in what is now Illinois. The trip covered about 1,400 miles and lasted 16 months.

During the Revolution, he met with General George Washington, offering to form a militia under his command, using Indian war tactics to harass the British. As a Colonel in the militia, he was instrumental in teaching the military Indian fighting tactics that are still implemented today.

At one point in his life, he was framed and tried for murder by vengeful traders, but was exonerated.

Smith journeyed to Missouri on a land scout with Daniel Morgan Boone and Joseph Scholl (Daniel Boones' son and son-in-law). No doubt, Smith was an acquaintance of Daniel as well.

He moved to Bourbon County, Kentucky. A very devout Christian, he preached at the famous Cane Ridge Revival just east of Paris/Lexington in 1801. (Cane Ridge was known as the most powerful Christian revival in America.) He was also a missionary to various Indian tribes, as he spoke several Indian dialects.

Smith's last military campaign was under Gen. Wm. Henry Harrison during the War of 1812. Smith was 74 years old. James Smith is surely one of America's unsung heroes!

AN ACCOUNT

OF THE

REMARKABLE OCCURRENCES

IN THE LIFE AND TRAVELS OF

Col. JAMES SMITH,

(Now a Citizen of Bourbon County, Kentucky,)

DURING HIS CAPTIVITY WITH THE INDIANS,

IN THE YEARS 1755, '56, '57, '58, & '59,

In which the Customs, Manners, Traditions, Theological Sentiments, Mode of Warfare, Military Tactics, Discipline and Encampments, Treatment of prisoners, &c. are better explained, and more minutely related, than has been heretofore done, by any author on that subject. Together with a Description of the Soil, Timber and Waters, where he travelled with the Indians, during his captivity.

TO WHICH IS ADDED,

A Brief Account of some Very Uncommon Occurrences, which transpired after his return from captivity; as well as of the Different Campaigns carried on against the Indians to the westward of Fort Pitt, since the year 1755, to the present date.

WRITTEN BY HIMSELF.

LEXINGTON:

PRINTED BY JOHN BRADFORD, ON MAIN STREET,

1799

COPYRIGHT SECURED ACCORDING TO ACT OF CONGRESS.

Printing Statement:

Due to the very old age and scarcity of this book, many of the pages may be hard to read due to the blurring of the original text, possible missing pages, missing text and other issues beyond our control.

Because this is such an important and rare work, we believe it is best to reproduce this book regardless of its original condition.

Thank you for your understanding.

PREFACE.

I WAS strongly urged to publish the following work, immediately after my return from captivity, which was nearly forty years ago – but, as at that time the Americans were so little acquainted with Indian affairs, I apprehended a great part of it would be viewed as fable or romance.

As the Indians never attempted to prevent me either from reading or writing, I kept a journal, which I revised shortly after my return from captivity, and which I have kept ever since; and as I have had but a moderate English education, have been advised to employ some person of liberal education to transcribe and embellish it – but believing that nature always outshines art, have thought, that occurrences truly and plainly stated, as they happened, would make the best history, be better understood, and most entertaining.

In the different Indian speeches copied into this work, I have not only imitated their own style, or mode of speaking, but have also preserved the ideas meant to be communicated in those speeches – In common conversation, I have used my own style, but preserved their ideas. The principal advantage that I expect will result to the public, from the publication of the following sheets, is the *observations on the Indian mode of warfare.* Experience has taught the Americans the necessity of adopting their mode, and the more perfect we are in that mode, the better we shall be able to defend ourselves against them, when defence is necessary.

JAMES SMITH.

Bourbon County, June 1st, 1799.

REMARKABLE

OCCURRENCES, &c.

IN May 1755, the province of Pennsylvania agreed to send out three hundred men, in order to cut a waggon road from Fort Loudon, to join Braddock's road, near the Turkey Foot, or three forks of Yohogania. My brother-in-law, William Smith esq. of Conococheague, was appointed commissioner, to have the oversight of these road-cutters.

Though I was at that time only eighteen years of age, I had fallen violently in love with a young lady, whom I apprehended was possessed of a large share of both beauty and virtue; but being born between Venus and Mars, I concluded I must also leave my dear fair one, and go out with this company of road-cutters, to see the event of this campaign; but still expecting that some time in the course of this summer, I should again return to the arms of my beloved.

We went on with the road, without interruption, until near the Allegheny Mountain, when I was sent back, in order to hurry up some provision waggons that were on the way after us. I proceeded down the road as far as the crossings of Juniata, where, finding the waggons were coming on as fast as possible, I returned up the road, again towards the Allegheny Mountain, in company with one Arnold Vigoras. About four or five miles above Bedford, three Indians had made a blind of bushes, stuck in the ground, as though they grew naturally, where they concealed themselves, about fifteen yards from the road. When we came opposite to them, they fired upon us, at this short distance, and killed my fellow traveler, yet their bullets did not touch me; but my horse, making a violent start, threw me, and the Indians immediately ran up and took me prisoner. The one that laid hold on me was a Canasatauga, the other two were Delawares. One of them could speak English and asked me if there were any more white men coming after? I told them not any near, that I knew of. Two of these

Indians stood by me, whilst the other scalped my comrade; they then set off and ran at a smart rate, through the woods, for about fifteen miles, and that night we slept on the Allegheny Mountain, without fire.

The next morning they divided the last of their provision which they had brought from Fort DuQuesne, and gave me an equal share, which was about two or three ounces of moldy biscuit – this and a young Ground Hog, about as large as a Rabbit, roasted, and also equally divided, was all the provision we had until we came to the Loyal-Hannan, which was about fifty miles; and a great part of the way we came through exceeding rocky Laurel-thickets, without any path. When we came to the West side of Laurel-Hill, they gave the scalp halloo, as usual, which is a long yell or halloo, for every scalp or prisoner they have in possession; the last of their scalp halloos were followed with quick and sudden, shrill shouts of joy and triumph. On their performing this, we were answered by the firing of a number of guns on the Loyal-Hannan, one after another, quicker than one could count, by another party of Indians, who were encamped near where Ligoneer now stands. As we advanced near this party, they increased with repeated shouts of joy and triumph; but I did not share with them in their excessive mirth. When we came to this camp, we found they had plenty of Turkeys and other meat there; and though I never before ate venison without bread or salt, yet as I was hungry, it relished very well. There we lay that night, and the next morning the whole of us marched on our way for Fort DuQuesne. The night after we joined another camp of Indians, with nearly the same ceremony, attended with great noise, and apparent joy, among all, except one. The next morning we continued our march, and in the afternoon, we came in full view of the fort, which stood on the point, near where Fort Pitt now stands. We then made a halt on the bank of the Allegheny, and repeated the scalp halloo, which was answered by the firing of all the firelocks in the hands of both Indians and French who were in and about the fort, in the aforesaid manner, and also the great guns, which were followed by the continued shouts and yells of the different savage tribes who were then collected there.

As I was at this time unacquainted with this mode of firing and yelling of the savages, I concluded there were thousands of Indians there, ready to receive General Braddock; but what added to my surprise, I saw numbers running towards me, stripped naked, excepting breech-clouts, and painted in the most hideous manner, of various colors, though the principal

color was vermillion, or a bright red; yet there was annexed to this, black, brown, blue, &c. As they approached, they formed themselves into two long ranks, about two or three rods apart. I was told by an Indian that could speak English, that I must run betwixt these ranks, and that they would flog me all the way as I ran, and if I ran quick, it would be so much the better, as they would quit when I got to the end of the ranks. There appeared to be a general rejoicing around me, yet, I could find nothing like joy in my breast; but I started to the race with all the resolution and vigor I was capable of exerting, and found that it was as I had been told, for I was flogged the whole way. When I got near the end of the lines, I was struck with something that appeared to me to be a stick, or the handle of a tommahawk, which caused me to fall to the ground. On my recovering my senses, I endeavored to renew my race; but as I arose, someone cast sand in my eyes, which blinded me so, that I could not see where to run. They continued beating me most intolerably, until I was at length insensible; but before I lost my senses, I remember my wishing them to strike the fatal blow, for I thought they intended killing me, but apprehended they were too long about it.

The first thing I remember was my being in the fort, amidst the French and Indians, and a French doctor standing by me, who had opened a vein in my left arm, after which the interpreter asked me how I did. I told him I felt much pain; the doctor then washed my wounds, and the bruised places of my body, with French brandy. As I felt faint, and the brandy smelt well, I asked for some inwardly, but the doctor told me, by the interpreter, that it did not suit my case.

When they found I could speak, a number of Indians came around me, and examined me with threats of cruel death, if I did not tell the truth. The first question they asked me was, how many men were there in the party that were coming from Pennsylvania to join Braddock? I told them the truth, that there were three hundred. The next question was, were they well armed? I told them they were all well armed (meaning the arm of flesh), for they had only about thirty guns among the whole of them, which, if the Indians had known, they would certainly have gone and cut them all off; therefore, I could not in conscience let them know the defenseless situation of these road-cutters. I was then sent to the hospital, and carefully attended by the doctors, and recovered quicker than what I expected.

Some time after I was there, I was visited by the Delaware Indian already mentioned, who was at the taking of me, and could speak some English. Though he spoke but bad English, yet I found him to be a man of considerable understanding. I asked him if I had done anything that had offended the Indians, which caused them to treat me so unmercifully? He said no, it was only an old custom the Indians had, and it was like how do you do; after that he said I would be well used. I asked him if I should be admitted to remain with the French? He said no – and told me that as soon as I recovered, I must not only go with the Indians, but must be made an Indian myself. I asked him what news from Braddock's army? He said the Indians spied them every day, and he shewed me by making marks on the ground with a stick, that Braddock's army was advancing in very close order, and that the Indians would surround them, take trees, and (as he expressed it) *shoot um down all one pigeon.*

Shortly after this, on the 9th day of July 1755, in the morning I heard a great stir in the fort. As I could then walk with a staff in my hand, I went out of the door which was just by the wall of the fort, and stood upon the wall and viewed the Indians in a huddle before the gate, where were barrels of powder, bullets, flints, &c. and every one taking what suited; I saw the Indians also march off in rank, entire – likewise the French Canadians, and some regulars; after viewing the Indians and French in different positions, I computed them to be about four hundred, and wondered that they attempted to go out against Braddock with so small a party. I was then in high hopes that I would soon see them flying before the British troops, and that General Braddock would take the fort and rescue me.

I remained anxious to know the event of this day; and in the afternoon I again observed a great noise and commotion in the fort, and though at that time I could not understand French, yet I found that it was the voice of joy and triumph, and feared that they had received what I called bad news.

I had observed some of the old country soldiers speak Dutch; as I spoke Dutch I went to one of them, and asked him what was the news? He told me that a runner had just arrived, who said that Braddock would certainly be defeated; that the Indians and French had surrounded him and were concealed behind trees and in gullies and kept a constant fire upon the English, and that they saw the English falling in heaps, and if they did not take the river which was the only gap, and make their escape, there would not be one man left alive before sun down. Some time after this I heard a number of scalp halloos and saw a company of Indians and French coming in. I observed they had a great many bloody scalps, grenadiers' caps, British canteens, bayonets, &c. with them. They brought the news that Braddock was defeated. After that another company came in which appeared to be about one hundred, and chiefly Indians, and it seemed to me that almost every one in this company was carrying scalps; after this came another company with a number of waggon-horses, and also a great many scalps. Those that were coming in, and those that had arrived, kept a constant firing of small arms, and also the great guns in the fort, which were accompanied with the most hideous shouts and yells from all quarters; so that it appeared to me as if the infernal regions had broke loose.

About sun down I beheld a small party coming in with about a dozen prisoners, stripped naked, with their hands tied behind their back, and their faces, and part of their bodies blacked – these prisoners they burned to death on the brink of Alegheny River opposite to the fort. I stood on the fort wall until I beheld them begin to burn one of these men; they had him tied to a stake and kept touching him with fire-brands, red-hot irons, &c. and he screeming in a most doleful manner – the Indians in the mean time yelling like infernal spirits. As this scene appeared too shocking for me to behold, I retired to my lodging both sore and sorry.

When I came into my lodgings I saw Russel's Seven Sermons, which they had brought from the field of battle, which a Frenchman made a present of to me. From the best information I could receive, there were only seven Indians and four French killed in this battle, and five hundred British lay dead in the field; besides what were killed in the river on their retreat.

The morning after the battle I saw Braddock's artilery brought into the fort, the same day I also saw several Indians in British-officers' dress with sash, half-moon, laced hats, &c. which the British then wore.

A few days after this the Indians demanded me and I was obliged to go with them. I was not yet well able to march, but they took me in a canoe, up the Alegheny River to an Indian town that was on the north side of the river, about forty miles above Fort DuQuesne. Here I remained about three weeks, and was then taken to an Indian town on the west branch of Muskingum, about twenty miles above the forks, which was called Tullihas, inhabited by Delawares, Caughnewagos and Mohicans. On our rout betwixt the aforesaid towns, the country was chiefly black-oak and white-oak land, which appeared generally to be good wheat land, chiefly second and third rate, intermixed with some rich bottoms.

The day after my arrival at the aforesaid town, a number of Indians collected about me, and one of them began to pull the hair out of my head. He had some ashes on a piece of

bark, in which he frequently diped his fingers in order to take the firmer hold, and so he went on, as if he had been plucking a turkey, until he had all the hair clean out of my head, except a small spot about three or four inches square on my crown; this they cut off with a pair of scissors, excepting three locks, which they dressed up in their own mode. Two of these they wraped round with a narrow beaded garter made by themselves for that purpose, and the other they platted at full length, and then stuck it full of silver broches. After this they bored my nose and ears, and fixed me off with ear rings and nose jewels, then they ordered me to strip off my clothes and put on a breech-clout, which

I did; they then painted my head, face and body in various colours. They put a large belt of wampum on my neck, and silver bands on my hands and right arm; and so an old chief led me out in the street and gave the alarm halloo, *coo-wigh*, several times repeated quick, and on this all that were in the town came running and stood round the old chief, who held me by the hand in the midst. As I at that time knew nothing of their mode of adoption, and had seen them put to death all they had taken, and as I never could find that they saved a man alive at Braddock's defeat, I made no doubt but they were about putting me to death in some cruel manner. The old chief holding me by the hand made a long speech very loud, and when he had done he handed me to three young squaws, who led me by the hand down the bank into the river until the water was up to our middle. The squaws then made signs to me to plunge myself into the water, but I did not understand them; I thought that the result of the council was that I should be drowned, and that these young ladies were to be the executioners. They all three laid violent hold of me, and I for some time opposed them with all my might, which occasioned loud laughter by the multitude that were on the bank of the river. At length one of the squaws made out to speak a little English (for I believe they began to be afraid of me) and said, *no hurt you*; on this I gave myself up to their ladyships, who were as good as their word; for though they plunged me under water, and washed and rubbed me severely, yet I could not say they hurt me much.

These young women then led me up to the council house, where some of the tribe were ready with new cloths for me. They gave me a new ruffled shirt, which I put on, also a pair of leggins done off with ribbons and beads, likewise a pair of mockasons, and garters dressed with beads, Porcupine-quills and redhair–also a tinsel laced cappo. They again painted my head and face with various colors, and tied a bunch of red feathers to one of these locks they had left on the crown of my head, which stood up five or six inches. They seated me on a bear skin, and gave me a pipe, tomahawk, and polecat skin pouch, which had been skinned pocket fashion, and contained tobacco, killegenico, or dry sumach leaves, which they mix with their tobacco, – also spunk, flint and steel. When I was thus seated, the Indians came in dressed and painted in their grandest manner. As they came in they took their seats and for a considerable time there was a profound silence, every one was smoking, – but not a word was spoken among them. – At length one of the chiefs made a speech which was delivered to me by an interpretor, – and was as followeth: – "My son, you are now flesh of our flesh, and bone of our bone. By the ceremony which was performed this day, every drop of white blood was washed out of your veins; you are taken into the Caughnewago nation, and initiated into a warlike tribe; you are adopted into a great family, and now received with great seriousness and solemnity in the room and place of a great man; after what has passed this day, you are now one of us by an old strong law and custom – My son, you have now nothing to fear, we are now under the same obligations to love, support and defend you, that we are to love and defend one another, therefore you are to consider yourself as one of our people." – At this time I did not believe this fine speech, especially that of the white blood being washed out of me, but since that time I have found that there was much sincerity in said speech, -- for from that day I never knew them to make any distinction between me and themselves in any respect whatever until I left them. – If they had plenty of cloathing I had plenty, if we were scarce we all shared one fate.

After this ceremony was over, I was introduced to my new kin, and told that I was to attend a feast that evening, which I did. And as the custom was, they gave me also a bowl and wooden spoon, which I carried with me to the place, where there was a number of large brass kettles full of boiled venison and green corn; every one advanced with his bowl and spoon and had his share given him. – After this one of the chiefs made a short speech, and then we began to eat.

The name of one of the chiefs in this town was Tecanyaterighto, alias Pluggy, and the other Asallecoa, alias Mohawk Soloman. – As Pluggy and his party were to start the next day to war, to the frontiers of Virginia, the next thing to be performed was the war dance, and their war songs. At their war dance, they had both vocal and instrumental music. They had a short holow gum close in one end, with water in it, and parchment stretched over the open end thereof, which they beat with one stick, and made a sound nearly like a muffled drum, -- all those, who were going on this expedition collected together and formed. An old Indian then began to sing, and timed the music by beating on this drum, as the ancients formerly timed their music by beating the tabor. On this the warriors began to advance, or move forward in concert, like well disciplined troops would march to the fife and drum. Each warrior had a tomahawk, spear or war-mallet in his hand, and they all moved regularly towards the call, or the way they intended to go to war. At length they all stretched their tomahawks towards the Potomack, and giving a hideous shout or yell, they wheeled quick about, and danced in the same manner back. The next was the war song. In performing this, only one sung at a time, in a moving posture, with a tomahawk in his hand, while all the other warriors were engaged in calling aloud *he-uh, he-uh,* which they constantly repeated, while the war song was going on. When the warrior that was singing had ended his song, he struck a war post with his tomahawk, and with a loud voice told what warlike exploits he had done, and what he now intended to do: which were answered by the other warriors, with loud shouts of applause. Some who had not before intended to go to war, at this time were so animated by this performance, that they took up the tomahawk and sung the war song, which was answered with shouts of joy, as they were then initiated into the present marching company. The next morning this company all collected at one place, with their heads and faces painted with various colors, and packs upon their backs: they marched off, all silent, except the commander, who, in the front sung the travelling song, which began in this manner: *"hoo caughtainte heegana"*. Just as the rear passed the end of the town, they began to fire in their slow manner, from the front to the rear, which was accompanied with shouts and yells from all quarters.

This evening I was invited to another sort of dance, which was a kind of promiscuous dance. The young men stood in one rank, and the young women in another, about one rod apart, facing each other. The one that raised the tune, or started the song, held a small gourd or dry shell of a squash, in his hand, which contained beads or small stones, which rattled. When he began to sing, he timed the tune with his rattle; both men and women danced and sung together, advancing towards each other, stooping until their heads would be touching together, and then ceased from dancing, with loud shouts, and retreated and formed again, and so repeated the same thing over and over, for three or four hours, without intermission. This exercise appeared to me at first, irrational and insipid; but I found that in singing their tunes, they used *ya ne no hoo wa ne*, &c. like our *fa sol la,* and though they have no such thing, as jingling verse, yet they can intermix sentences with their notes, and say what they please to each other, and carry on the tune in concert. I found that this was a kind of wooing, or courting dance, and as they advanced stooping with their heads together, they could say what they pleased in each other's ear, without disconcerting their rough music, and the others, or those near, not hear what they say.

Shortly after this I went out to hunt, in company with Mohawk Solomon, some of the Caughnewagas and a Delaware Indian that was married to a Caughnewaga squaw. We travelled about south, from this town, and the first night we killed nothing, but we had with us green corn, which we roasted and ate that night. The next day we encamped about twelve o'clock, and the hunters turned out to hunt, and I went down the run that we encamped on, in company with some squaws and boys, to hunt plumbs, which we found in great plenty. On my return to camp I observed a large piece of fat meat: the Delaware Indian that could talk some English, observed me looking earnestly at this meat, and asked me *what meat you think that is?* I said I supposed it was bear meat; he laughed and said, *ho, all one fool you, beal now elly pool,* and pointing to the other side of the camp, he said *look at that skin, you think that beal skin?* I went and lifted the skin, which appeared like an ox hide: he then said, *what skin you think that?* I replied that I thought it was a buffaloe hide; he laughed and said *you fool again, you know nothing, you think buffaloe that colo?* I acknowledged I did not know much about these things, and told him I never saw a buffaloe, and that I had not heard what color they were. He replyed *by and by you shall see gleat many buffaloe; He now go to gleat lick. That skin no buffaloe skin, that skin buck-elk skin.* They went out with horses, and brought in the remainder of this buck-elk, which was the fattest creature I ever saw of the tallow kind.

We remained at this camp about eight or ten days, and killed a number of deer. Though we had neither bread or salt at this time, yet we had both roast and boiled meat in great plenty, and they were frequently inviting me to eat, when I had no appetite.

We then moved to the buffaloe lick, where we killed several buffaloe, and in their small brass kettles they made about half a bushel of salt. I suppose this lick was about thirty or forty miles from the aforesaid town, and somewhere between the Muskinguin, Ohio and Sciota. About the lick was clear, open woods, and thin white-oak land, and at that time there were large roads leading to the lick, like waggon roads. We moved from this lick about six or seven miles, and encamped on a creek.

Though the Indians had given me a gun, I had not yet been admitted to go out from the camp to hunt. At this place Mohawk Solomon asked me to go out with him to hunt, which I readily agreed to. After some time we came upon some fresh buffaloe tracks. I had observed before this that the Indians were upon their guard, and afraid of an enemy, for, until now they and the southern nations had been at war. As we were following the buffaloe tracks, Solomon seemed to be upon his guard, went very slow, and would frequently stand and listen, and appeared to be in suspense. We came to where the tracks were very plain in the sand, and I said it is surely buffaloe tracks: he said *hush, you know nothing, may be buffaloe tracks, may be Catawba..* He went very cautious until we found some fresh buffaloe dung: he then smiled, and said *Catawba can not make so.* He then stopped and told me an odd story about the Catawbas. He said that formerly the Catawbas came near one of their hunting camps, and at some distance from the camp lay in ambush, and in order to decoy them out, sent two or three Catawbas in the night, past their camp, with buffaloe hoofs fixed on their feet, so as to make artificial tracks. In the morning those in the camp followed after these tracks, thinking they were buffaloe, until they were fired on by the Catawbas, and several of them killed; the others fled, collected a party and pursued the Catawbas; but they (the Catawbas) in their subtlety brought with them rattle-snake poison, which they had collected from the bladder that lieth at the root of the snakes' teeth; this they had corked up in a short piece of a cane-stalk; they had also brought with them small cane or reed, about the size of a rye straw, which they made sharp at the end like a pen, and dipped them in this poison, and stuck them in the ground among the grass, along their own tracks, in such a position that they might stick into the legs of the pursuers, which answered the design; and as the Catawbas had runners behind to watch the motions of the pursuers, when they found that a number of them were lame, being artificially snake bit, and that they were all turning back, the Catawbas turned upon the pursuers, and defeated them, and killed and scalped all those that were lame. --- When Solomon had finished this story, and found that I understood him, concluded by saying, *you don't know, Catawba velly bad Indian, Catawba all one Devil Catawba.*

Some time after this, I was told to take the dogs with me and go down the creek, perhaps I might kill a turkey; it being in the afternoon, I was also told not to go far from the creek, and to come up the creek again to the camp, and to take care not to get lost. When I had gone some distance down the creek, I came upon fresh buffaloe tracks, and as I had a number of dogs with me to stop the buffaloe, I concluded I would follow after and kill one; and as the grass and weeds were rank, I could readily follow the track. A little before sundown, I despaired of coming up with them: I was then thinking how I might get to camp before night; I concluded as the buffaloe had made several turns, if I took the track back to the creek, it would be dark before I could get to camp; therefore I thought I would take a near way through the hills, and strike the creek a little below the camp; but as it was cloudy weather, and I a very young woodsman, I could find neither creek or camp. When night came on, I fired my gun several times, and hallooed; but could have no answer. The next morning early, the Indians were out after me, and as I had with me ten or a dozen dogs, and the grass and weeds rank, they could readily follow my track. When they came up with me, they appeared to be in a very good humor. I asked Solomon if he thought I was running away, he said *no no, you go too much clooked.* On my return to camp they took my gun from me, and for this rash step I was reduced to a bow and arrows, for near two years. We were out on this tour about six weeks.

This country is generally hilly, though intermixed with considerable quantities of rich upland, and some good bottoms.

When we returned to the town, Pluggy and his party had arrived, and brought with them a considerable number of scalps and prisoners from the South Branch of Potomack: they also brought with them an English Bible, which they gave to a Dutch woman who was a prisoner; but as she could not read English, she made a present of it to me, which was very acceptable.

I remained in this town until some time in October, when my adopted brother, called Tontileaugo, who had married a Wiandot squaw, took me with him to Lake Erie. We proceeded up the west branch of Muskingum, and for some distance up the river the land was hilly but intermixed with large bodies of tolerable rich upland, and excellent bottoms. We proceeded on, to the head waters of the west branch of Muskingum. On the head waters of this branch, and from thence to the waters of Canesadooharie, there is a large body of rich, well lying land – the timber is ash, walnut, sugar-tree, buckeye, honey-locust and cherry, intermixed with some oak, hickory, &c. This tour was at the time that the black-haws were ripe, and we were seldom out of sight of them; they were common here both in the bottoms and upland.

On this route we had no horses with us, and when we started from the town, all the pack I carried was a pouch, containing my books, a little dried venison, and my blanket. I had then no gun, but Tontileaugo who was a first-rate hunter, carried a rifle gun, and every day killed deer, racoons or bears. We left the meat, excepting a little for present use, and carried the skins with us until we encamped, and then stretched them with elm bark, in a frame made with poles stuck in the ground and tied together with lynn or elm bark; and when the skins were dried by the fire, we packed them up, and carried them with us the next day.

As Tontileaugo could not speak English, I had to make use of all the Caughnewaga I had learned even to talk very imperfectly with him; but I found I learned to talk Indian faster this way, than when I had those with me who could speak English.

As we proceeded down the Canesadooharie waters, our packs encreased by the skins that were daily killed, and became so very heavy that we could not march more than eight or ten miles per day. We came to Lake Erie about six miles west of the mouth of Canesadooharie. As the wind was very high the evening we came to the Lake, I was surprized to hear the roaring of the water, and see high waves that dashed against the shore, like the Ocean. We encamped on a run near the lake; and as the wind fell that night, the next morning the lake was only in a moderate motion, and we marched on the land along the side of the water, frequently resting ourselves, as we were heavy laden. I saw on the strand, a number of large fish, that had been left in flat or hollow places; as the wind fell and the waves abated, they were left without water, or only a small quantity; and numbers of Bald and Grey Eagles, &c. were along the shore devouring them.

Some time in the afternoon we came to a large camp of Wiandots, at the mouth of Canesadooharie, where Tontileaugo's wife was. Here we were kindly received: they gave us a kind of rough, brown potatoes, which grew spontaneously and is called by the Caughnewagas *ohnenata.* These potatoes peeled and dipped in racoons' fat, taste nearly like our sweet-potatoes. They also gave us what they call *caneheanta*, which is a kind of homony, made of green corn, dried, and beans mixed together.

From the head waters of Canesadooharie to this place, the land is generally good; chiefly first or second rate, and, comparatively, little or no third rate. The only refuse is some swamps, that appear to be too wet for use, yet I apprehend that a number of them, if drained, would make excellent meadows. The timber is black-oak, walnut, hickory, cherry, black-ash, white-ash, water-ash, buckeye, black-locust, honey-locust, sugar-tree and elm: there is also some land, though, comparatively, but small, where the timber is chiefly white-oak or beach – this may be called third rate. In the bottoms, and also many places in the upland, there is a large quantity of wild apple, plumb, and red and black-haw trees. It appeared to be well watered, and a plenty of meadow ground, intermixed with upland, but no large prairies or glades, that I saw, or heard of. In this route, deer, bear, turkeys and racoons, appeared plenty, but no buffaloe, and very little sign of elks.

We continued our camp at the mouth of Canesadooharie for some time, where we killed some deer, and a great many racoons; the racoons here were remarkably large and fat. At length we all embarked in a large birch bark canoe. This vessel was about four feet wide, and three feet deep, and about five and thirty feet long: and tho it could carry a heavy burden, it was so artfully and curiously constructed that four men could cary it several miles, or from one landing place to another, or from the waters of the Lake to the waters of the Ohio. We proceeded up Canesadooharie a few miles and went on shore to hunt; but to my great surprise, they carried the vessel that we all came in up the bank, and inverted it or turned the bottom up, and converted it to a dwelling house, and kindled a fire before us to warm ourselves by and cook. With our baggage and ourselves in this house we were very much crouded, yet our little house turned off the rain very well.

We kept moving and hunting up this river until we came to the falls; here we remained some weeks, and killed a number of deer, several bears, and a great many racoons. From the mouth of this river to the falls is about five and twenty miles. On our passage up I was not much out from the river, but what I saw was good land, and not hilly.

About the falls is thin chesnut land, which is almost the only chesnut timber I ever saw in this country.

While we remained here, I left my pouch with my books in camp, wrapt up in my blanket, and went out to hunt chestnuts. On my return to camp my books were missing. I enquired after them, and asked the Indians if they knew where they were; they told me that they supposed the puppies had carried them off. I did not believe them; but thought they were displeased at my poring over my books, and concluded that they had destroyed them, or put them out of my way.

After this I was again out after nuts, and on my return beheld a new erection, which were two white oak saplings, that were forked about twelve feet high, and stood about fifteen feet apart. They had cut these saplings at the forks and laid a strong pole across which appeared in the form of a gallows, and the posts they had shaved very smooth and painted in places with vermilion. I could not conceive the use of this piece of work; and at length concluded it was a gallows, I thought that I had displeased them by reading my books, and that they were about putting me to death. The next morning I observed them bringing their skins all to this place and hanging them over this pole, so as to preserve them from being injured by the weather; this removed my fears. They also buried their large canoe in the ground, which is the way they took to preserve this fort of a canoe in the winter season.

As we had at this time no horses, every one got a pack on his back, and we steered an east course about twelve miles, and encamped. The next morning we proceeded on the same course about ten miles to a large creek that empties into Lake Erie betwixt Canesadooharie and Cayahaga. Here they made their winter cabbin, in the following form. They cut logs about fifteen feet long, and laid these logs upon each other, and drove posts in the ground at each end to keep them together; the posts they tied together at the top with bark, and by this means raised a wall fifteen feet long, and about four feet high, and in the same manner they raised another wall opposite to this, at about twelve feet distance; then they drove forks in the ground in the centre of each end, and laid a strong pole from end to end on these forks; and from these walls to the poles, they set up poles instead of rafters, and on these they tied small poles in place of laths; and a cover was made of lynn bark which will run even in the winter season.

As every tree will not run, they examine the tree first, by trying it near the ground, and when they find it will do, they fall the tree and raise the bark with the tomahawk, near the top of the tree about five or six inches broad, then put the tomahawk handle under this bark, and pull it along down to the butt of the tree; so that some times one piece of bark will be thirty feet long; this bark they cut at suitable lengths in order to cover the hut.

At the end of these walls they set up split timber, so that they had timber all round, excepting a door at each end. At the top, in place of a chimney, they left an open place, and for bedding they laid down the aforesaid kind of bark, on which they spread bear skins. From end to end of this hut along the middle there were fires, which the squaws made of dry split wood, and the holes or open places that appeared, the squaws stopped with moss, which they collected from old logs; and at the door they hung a bear skin; and notwithstanding the winters are hard here, our lodging was much better than what I expected.

It was some time in December when we finished this winter cabbin, but when we had got into this comparatively fine lodging, another difficulty arose; we had nothing to eat. While I was travelling with Tontileaugo, as was before mentioned, and had plenty of fat venison, bears meat and racoons, I then thought it was hard living without bread or salt; but now I began to conclude, that if I had any thing that would banish pinching hunger, and keep soul and body together I would be content.

While the hunters were all out, exerting themselves to the utmost of their ability, the squaws and boys (in which class I was) were scattered out in the bottoms, hunting red-haws, black-haws and hickory-nuts. As it was too late in the year, we did not succeed in gathering haws; but we had tolerable success in scratching up hickory-nuts from under a light snow, which we carried with us lest the hunters should not succeed. After our return the hunters came in, who had killed only two small turkeys, which were but little among eight hunters and thirteen squaws, boys and children; but they were divided with the greatest equity and justice – every one got their equal share.

The next day the hunters turned out again, and killed one deer and three bears.

One of the bears was very large and remarkably fat. The hunters carried in meat sufficient to give us all a hearty supper and breakfast.

The squaws and all that could carry turned out to bring in meat – every one had their share assigned them, and my load was among the least; yet, not being accustomed to carrying in this way, I got exceeding weary, and told them my load was too heavy, I must leave part of it and come for it again. They made a halt and only laughed at me, and took part of my load and added it to a young squaw's, who had as much before as I carried.

This kind of reproof had a greater tendency to excite me to exert myself in carrying without complaining, than if they had whipped me for laziness. After this the hunters held a council, and concluded that they must have horses to carry their loads; and that they would go to war even in this inclement season, in order to bring in horses.

Tontileaugo wished to be one of those who should go to war; but the votes went against him; as he was one of our best hunters; it was thought necessary to leave him at this winter camp to provide for the squaws and children; it was agreed upon that Tontileaugo and three others should stay and hunt, and the other four go to war.

They then began to go through their common ceremony. They sung their war songs, danced their war dances, &c. And when they were equipped they went off singing their marching song, and firing their guns. Our camp appeared to be rejoicing, but I was grieved to think that some innocent persons would be murdered, not thinking of danger.

After the departure of these warriors, we had hard times and tho we were not altogether out of provisions, we were brought to short allowance. At length Tontileaugo had a considerable success; and we had meat brought into camp sufficient to last ten days. Tontileaugo then took me with him in order to encamp some distance from this winter cabbin, to try his luck there. We carried no provision with us, he said we would leave what was there for the squaws and children, and that we could shift for ourselves. We steered about a south course up the waters of this creek, and encamped about ten or twelve miles from the winter cabbin. As it was still cold weather and a crust upon the snow, which made a noise as we walked and alarmed the deer, we could kill nothing, and consequently went to sleep without supper. The only chance we had under these circumstances, was to hunt bear holes; as the bears about Christmas search out a winter lodging place, where they lie about three or four months without eating or drinking – This may appear to some incredible; but it is now well known to be the case, by those who live in the remote western parts of North America.

The next morning early we proceeded on, and when we found a tree scratched by the bears climbing up, and the hole in the tree sufficiently large for the reception of the bear, we then fell a sapling or small tree, against or near the hole; and it was my business to climb up and drive out the bear, while Tontileaugo stood ready with his gun and bow. We went on in this manner until evening, without success; at length we found a large elm scratched, and a hole in it about forty feet up; but no tree nigh suitable to lodge against the hole. Tontileaugo got a long pole and some dry rotten wood which he tied in bunches, with bark, and as there was a tree that grew near the elm, and extended up near the hole, but leaned the wrong way, so that we could not lodge it to advantage; but to remedy this inconvenience, he climed up this tree and carried with him his rotten wood, fire and pole. The rotten wood he tied to his belt, and to one end of the pole he tied a hook, and a piece of rotten wood which he set fire to, as it would retain fire almost like spunk; and reached this hook from limb to limb as he went up; when he got up, with this pole he put dry wood on fire into the hole, after he put in the fire he heard the bear snuff and he came speedily down, took his gun in his hand and waited until the bear would come out; but it was some time before it appeared, and, when it did appear, he attempted taking sight with his rifle; but it being then too dark, to see the sights, he set it down by a tree, and instantly bent his bow, took hold of an arrow, and shot the bear a little behind the shoulder; I was preparing also to shoot an arrow, but he called to me to stop, there was no occasion, and with that the bear fell to the ground.

Being very hungry we kindled a fire, opened the bear, took out the liver, and wrapped some of the caul fat round and put it on a wooden spit which we stuck in the ground by the fire to roast, we then skinned the bear, got on our kettle, and had both roast and boiled, and also sauce to our meat, which appeared to me to be delicate fare. After I was fully satisfied I went to sleep, Tontileaugo awoke me, saying, come eat hearty, we have got meat plenty now.

The next morning we cut down a lynn tree, peeled bark and made a snug little shelter, facing the south east, with a large log betwixt us and the north west; we made a good fire before us, and scaffolded up our meat at one side. When we had finished our camp we went out to hunt, searched two trees for bears, but to no purpose. As the snow thawed a little in the afternoon Tontileaugo killed a deer, which we carried with us to camp.

The next day we turned out to hunt, and near the camp we found a tree well scratched; but the hole was above forty feet high, and no tree that we could lodge against the hole; but finding that it was very hollow, we concluded that we would cut down the tree with our tomahawks, which kept us working a considerable part of the day. When the tree fell we ran up, Tontileaugo with his gun and bow, and I with my bow ready bent. Tontileaugo shot the bear through with his rifle, a little behind the shoulders; I also shot, but too far back; and not being then much accustomed to the business, my arrow penetrated only a few inches thro the skin. Having killed an old she bear and three cubs, we hawled her on the snow to the camp, and only had time afterwards, to get wood, make a fire, cook, &c. before dark.

Early the next morning we went to business, searched several trees, but found no bears. On our way home we took three racoons out of a hollow elm, not far from the ground.

We remained here about two weeks, and in this time killed four bears, three deer, several turkeys, and a number of racoons. We packed up as much meat as we could carry, and returned to our winter cabbin. On our arrival, there was great joy, as they were all in a starving condition – the three hunters that we had left having killed but very little. All that could carry a pack repaired to our camp to bring in meat.

Some time in February the four warriors returned, who had taken two scalps, and six horses from the frontiers, of Pennsylvania. The hunters could then scatter out a considerable distance from the winter cabbin, and encamp, kill meat and pack it in upon horses; so that we commonly after this had plenty of provision.

In this month we began to make sugar. As some of the elm bark will strip at this season, the squaws after finding a tree that would do, cut it down, and with a crooked stick broad and sharp at the end, took the bark off the tree, and of this bark, made vessels in a curious manner, that would hold about two gallons each; they made above one hundred of these kind of vessels. In the sugar-tree they cut a notch, slooping down, and at the end of the notch, stuck in a tomahawk; in the place where they stuck the tomahawk, they drove a long chip, in order to carry the water out from the tree, and under this they set their vessel, to receive it. As sugar trees were plenty and large here, they seldom or never notched a tree that was not two or three feet over. They also made bark vessels for carrying the water, that would hold about four gallons each. They had two brass kettles, that held about fifteen gallons each, and other smaller kettles in which they boiled the water. But as they could not at all times boil away the water as fast as it was collected, they made vessels of bark, that would hold about one hundred gallons each, for retaining the water; and tho' the sugar trees did not run every day, they had always a sufficient quantity of water to keep them boiling during the whole sugar season.

The way that we commonly used our sugar while encamped, was by putting it in bears fat until the fat was almost as sweet as the sugar itself, and in this we dipped our roasted venison. About this time some of the Indian lads and myself, were employed in making and attending traps for catching racoons, foxes, wild cats, &c.

As the racoon is a kind of water animal, that frequents the runs, or small water-courses, almost the whole night, we made our traps on the runs, by laying one small sapling on another, and driving in posts to keep them from rolling. The upper sapling we raised about eighteen inches, and set so, that on the racoons touching a string, or small piece of bark, the sapling would fall and kill it; and lest the racoon should pass by, we laid brush on both sides of the run, only leaving the channel open.

The fox traps we made nearly in the same manner, at the end of a hollow log, or opposite to a hole at the root of a hollow tree, and put venison on a stick for bait: we had it so set that when the fox took hold of the meat, the trap fell. While the squaws were employed in making sugar, the boys and men were engaged in hunting and trapping.

About the latter end of March we began to prepare for moving into town, in order to plant corn: the squaws were then frying the last of their bears fat, and making vessels to hold it: the vessels were made of deer skins, which were skinned by pulling the skin off the neck, without ripping. After they had taken off the hair, they gathered it in small plaits round the neck and with a string drew it together like a purse: in the centre a pin was put, below which they tied a string, and while it was wet they blew it up like a bladder, and let it remain in this manner, until it was dry, when it appeared nearly in the shape of a sugar loaf, but more rounding at the lower end. One of these vessels would hold about four or five gallons; in these vessels it was they carried their bears oil.

When all things were ready we moved back to the falls of Canesadooharie. In this route the land is chiefly first and second rate, but too much meadow ground, in proportion to the up land. The timber is white ash, elm, black-oak, cherry, buckeye, sugar-tree, lynn, mulberry, beech, white-oak, hickory, wild apple-tree, red-haw, black-haw, and spicewood bushes. There is in some places, spots of beech timber, which spots may be called third rate land. Buckeye, sugar-tree and spicewood, are common in the woods here. There is in some places, large swamps too wet for any use.

On our arrival at the falls, (as we had brought with us on horse back, about two hundred weight of sugar, a large quantity of bears oil, skins &c.) the canoe we had buried was not sufficient to carry all; therefore we were obliged to make another one of elm bark. While we lay here a young Wiandot found my books: on this they collected together; I was a little way from the camp, and saw the collection, but did not know what it meant. They called me by my Indian name, which was Scoouwa, repeatedly. I ran to see what was the matter, they shewed me my books, and said they were glad they had been found, for they knew I was grieved at the loss of them, and that they now rejoiced with me because they were found. As I could then speak some Indian, especially Caughnewaga (for both that and the Wiandot tongue were spoken in this camp) I told them that I thanked them for the kindness they had always shewn to me, and also for finding my books. They asked if the books were damaged? I told them not much. They then shewed how they lay, which was in the best manner to turn off the water. In a deer skin pouch they lay all winter. The print was not much injured, though the binding was. – This was the first time that I felt my heart warm towards the Indians. Though they had been exceeding kind to me, I still before detested them, on account of the barbarity I beheld after Braddock's defeat. Neither had I ever before pretended kindness, or expressed myself in a friendly manner; but I began now to excuse the Indians on account of their want of information.

When we were ready to embark, Tontileaugo would not go to town, but go up the river and take a hunt. He asked me if I choosed to go with him? I told him I did. We then got some sugar, bears oil bottled up in a bear's gut, and some dry venison, which we packed up, and went up Canesadooharie, about thirty miles, and encamped. At this time I did not know either the day of the week, or the month; but I supposed it to be about the first of April. We had considerable success in our business. We also found some stray horses, or a horse, mare, and a young colt; and though they had run in the woods all winter, they were in exceeding good order. There is plenty of grass here all winter, under the snow, and horses accustomed to the woods can work it out. – These horses had run in the woods until they were very wild.

Tontileaugo one night concluded that we must run them down. I told him I thought we could not accomplish it. He said he had run down bears, buffaloes and elks: and in the great plains, with only a small snow on the ground, he had run down a deer; and he thought that in one whole day, he could tire, or run down any four footed animal except a wolf. I told him that though a deer was the swiftest animal to run a short distance, yet it would tire sooner than a horse. He said he would at all events try the experiment. He had heard the Wiandots say, that I could run well, and now he would see whether I could or not. I told him that I never had run all day, and of course was not accustomed to that way of running. I never had run with the Wiandots, more than seven or eight miles at one time. He said that was nothing, we must either catch these horses, or run all day.

In the morning early we left camp, and about sunrise we started after them, stripped naked excepting breech-clouts and mockasons. About ten o'clock I lost sight of both Tontileaugo and the horses, and did not see them again until about three o'clock in the afternoon. As the horses run all day, in about three or four miles square, at length they passed where I was, and I fell in close after them. As I then had a long rest, I endeavored to keep ahead of Tontileaugo, and after some time I could hear him after me calling *chakoh, chakoanaugh*, which signifies, pull away or do your best. We pursued on, and after some time Tontileaugo passed me, and about an hour before sundown, we despaired of catching these horses and returned to camp where we had left our clothes.

I reminded Tontileaugo of what I had told him; he replied he did not know what horses could do. They are wonderful strong to run; but withal we made them very tired. Tontileaugo then concluded, he would do as the Indians did with wild horses, when out at war: which is to shoot them through the neck under the mane, and above the bone, which will cause them to fall and lie until they can halter them, and then they recover again. This he attempted to do; but as the mare was very wild, he could not get sufficiently nigh to shoot her in the proper place; however he shot, the ball passed too low, and killed her. As the horse and colt stayed at this place, we caught the horse, and took him and the colt with us to camp.

We stayed at this camp about two weeks, and killed a number of bears, racoons, and some beavers. We made a canoe of elm bark, and Tontileaugo embarked in it. He arrived at the falls that night; whilst I, mounted on horse back, with a bear skin saddle, and bark stirrups, proceeded by land to the falls: I came there the next morning, and we carried our canoe and loading past the falls.

The river is very rapid for some distance above the falls, which are about twelve or fifteen feet nearly perpendicular. This river, called Canesadooharie, interlocks with the West branch of Muskingum, runs nearly a north course, and empties into the south side of Lake Erie, about eighty miles east from Sandusky, or betwixt Sandusky and Cayahaga.

On this last route the land is nearly the same, as that last described, only there is not so much swampy or wet ground.

We again proceeded towards the lake, I on horse back, and Tontileaugo by water. Here the land is generally good, but I found some difficulty in getting round swamps and ponds. When we came to the lake I proceeded along the strand, and Tontileaugo near the shore, sometimes paddling and sometimes polling his canoe along.

After some time the wind arose, and he went into the mouth of a small creek and encamped. Here we staid several days on account of high wind, which raised the lake in great billows. While we were here Tontileaugo went out to hunt, and when he was gone a Wiandot came to our camp; I gave him a shoulder of venison which I had by the fire well roasted, and he received it gladly, told me he was hungry, and thanked me for my kindness. When Tontileaugo came home, I told him that a Wiandot had been at camp, and that I gave him a shoulder of roasted venison: he said that was very well, and I suppose you gave him also sugar and bears oil, to eat with his venison. I told him I did not; as the sugar and bears oil was down in the canoe I did not go for it. He replied you have behaved just like a Dutchman.* Do you not know that when strangers come to our camp, we ought always to give them the best that we have? I acknowledged that I was wrong. He said that he could excuse this, as I was but young; but I must learn to behave like a warrior, and do great things, and never be found in any such little actions.

The lake being again calm,** we proceeded, and arrived safe at Sunyendeand, which was a Wiandot town, that lay upon a small creek which empties into the Little Lake below the mouth of Sandusky.

The town was about eighty rods above the mouth of the creek on the south side of a large plain, on which timber grew, and nothing more but grass and nothing more but grass or nettles. In some places there were large flats, where nothing but grass grew, about three feet high when grown, and in other places nothing but nettles, very rank, where the soil is extremely rich and loose – here they planted corn. In this town there were also French traders, who purchased our skins and fur, and we all got new clothes, paint, tobacco, &c.

After I had got my new clothes, and my head done off like a red-headed wood-pecker, I, in company with a number of young Indians, went down to the corn field, to see the squaws at work. When we came there, they asked me to take a hoe, which I did, and hoed for some time. The squaws applauded me as a good hand at the business; but when I returned to the town, the old men hearing of what I had done, chid me, and said that I was adopted in the place of a great man, and must not hoe corn like a squaw. They never had occasion to reprove me for any thing like this again; as I never was extremely fond of work, I readily complied with their orders.

As the Indians on their return from their winter hunt, bring in with them large quantities of bears oil, sugar, dried venison, &c. at this time they have plenty, and do not spare eating or giving – thus they make way with their provision as quick as possible. They have no such thing as regular meals, breakfast, dinner or supper; but if any one, even the town folks, would go to the same house, several times in one day, he would be invited to eat of the best – and with them it is bad manners to refuse to eat when it is offered. If they will not eat it is

---

* The Dutch he called Skoharehaugo, which took its derivation from a Dutch settlement called Skoharey.
** The Iske when calm, appears to be of a sky blue colour; though when lifted in a vessel, it is like other clear water.

interpreted as a symptom of displeasure, or that the persons refusing to eat, were angry with those who invited them.

At this time homony plentifully mixed with bears' oil and sugar; or dried venison, bears oil and sugar, is what they offer to every one who comes in any time of the day; and so they go on until their sugar, bears oil and venison, is all gone, and then they have to eat homony by itself, without bread, salt or any thing else; yet, still they invite every one that comes in, to eat whilst they have any thing to give. It is thought a shame, not to invite people to eat, while they have any thing; but, if they can in truth, only say we have got nothing to eat, this is accepted as a honorable apology. All the hunters and warriors continued in town about six weeks after we came in: they spent this time in painting, going from house to house, eating, smoking and playing at a game resembling dice, or hustle-cap. They put a number of plumb-stones in a small bowl; one side of each stone is black, and the other white; they then shake or hustle the bowl, calling, *hits, hits, hits, honesey, honesey, rago, rago*; which signifies calling for white or black, or what they wish to turn up; they then turn the bowl, and count the whites and blacks. Some were beating their kind of drum, and singing; others were employed in playing on a sort of flute, made of hollow cane; and others playing on the jews-harp. Some part of this time was also taken up in attending the council house, where the chiefs, and as many others as chose, attended; and at night they were frequently employed in singing and dancing. Towards the last of this time, which was in June 1756, they were all engaged in preparing to go to war against the frontiers of Virginia: when they were equipped, they went through their ceremonies, sung their war songs, &c. They all marched off, from fifteen to sixty years of age; and some boys only twelve years old, were equipped with their bows and arrows, and went to war; so that none were left in town but squaws and children, except myself, one very old man, and another about fifty years of age, who was lame.

The Indians were then in great hopes that they would drive all the Virginians over the lake, which is all the name they know for the sea. They had some cause for this hope, because, at this time, the Americans were altogether unacquainted with war of any kind, and consequently very unfit to stand their hand with such subtil enemies as the Indians were. The two old Indians asked me if I did not think that the Indians and French would subdue all America, except New-England, which they said they had tried in old times. I told them I thought not: they said they had already drove them all of out of the mountains, and had chiefly laid waste the great valley, betwixt the

North and South mountain, from Potomack to James River, which is a considerable part of the best land in Virginia, Maryland and Pennsylvania, and that the white people appeared to them like fools; they could neither guard against surprize, run or fight. These they said were their reasons for saying that they would subdue the whites. They asked me to offer my reasons for my opinion, and told me to speak my mind freely. I told them that the white people to the East were very numerous, like the trees, and though they appeared to them to be fools, as they were not acquainted with their way of war, yet they were not fools; therefore after some time they will learn your mode of war, and turn upon you, or at least defend themselves. I found that the old men themselves did not believe they could conquer America, yet they were willing to propagate the idea, in order to encourage the young men to go to war.

When the warriors left this town we had neither meat sugar or bears oil, left. All that we had then to live on was corn pounded into coarse meal or small homony – this they boiled in water, which appeared like well thickened soup, without salt or any thing else. For some time, we had plenty of this kind of homony; at length we were brought to very short allowance, and as the warriors did not return as soon as they expected, we were in a starving condition, and but one gun in the town, and very little amunition. The old lame Wiandot concluded that he would go a hunting in a canoe, and take me with him, and try to kill deer in the water, as it was then watering time. We went up Sandusky a few miles, then turned up a creek, and encamped. We had lights prepared, as we were to hunt in the night, and also a piece of bark, and some bushes set up in the canoe, in order to conceal ourselves from the deer. A little boy that was with us, held the light, I worked the canoe, and the old man, who had his gun loaded with large shot, when we came near the deer, fired, and in this manner killed three deer, in part of one night. We went to our fire, ate heartily, and in the morning returned to town, in order to relieve the hungry and distressed.

When we came to town, the children were crying bitterly on account of pinching hunger. We delivered what we had taken, and though it was but little among so many, it was divided according to the strictest rules of justice. We immediately set out for another hunt, but before we returned a part of the warriors had come in, and brought with them on horse back, a quantity of meat. These warriors had divided into different parties, and all struck at different places in Augusta county. They brought in with them a considerable number of scalps, prisoners, horses, and other plunder. One of the parties brought in with them, one Arthur Campbell, that is now Col. Campbell, who lives on Holston River, near the Royal-Oak. As the Wiandots at Sunyendeand, and those at Detroit were connected, Mr. Campbell was taken to Detroit; but he remained some time with me in this town: his company was very agreeable, and I was sorry when he left me. During his stay at Sunyendeand he borrowed my Bible, and made some pertinent remarks on what he had read. One passage was where it is said, "It is good for a man that he bear the yoke in his youth." He said we ought to be resigned to the will of Providence, as we were now bearing the yoke, in our youth. Mr. Campbell appeared to be then about sixteen or seventeen years of age.

There was a number of prisoners brought in by these parties and when they were to run the gauntlet, I went and told them how they were to act. One John Savage, was brought in, a middle aged man, or about forty years old. He was to run the gauntlet. I told him what he had to do; and after this I fell into one of the ranks with the Indians, shouting and yelling like them, and as they were not very severe on him, as he passed me, I hit him with a piece of a pumpkin—which pleased the Indians much, but hurt my feelings.

About the time that these warriors came in, the green corn was beginning to be of use; so that we had either green corn or venison, and sometimes both—which was comparatively, high living. When we could have plenty of green corn, or roasting-ears, the hunters became lazy, and spent their time as already mentioned, in singing and dancing &c. They appeared to be fulfilling the scriptures beyond those who profess to believe them, in that of taking no thought of to-morrow: and also in living in love, peace and friendship together, without disputes. In this respect, they shame those who profess Christianity.

In this manner we lived, until October, then the geese, swans, ducks, cranes, &c. came from the north, and alighted on this little Lake, without number or innumerable. Sunyendeand is a remarkable place for fish, in the spring, and fowl both in the fall and spring.

As our hunters were now tired with indolence, and fond of their own kind of exercise, they all turned out to fowling, and in this could scarce miss of success; so that we had now plenty of homony and the best of fowls; and sometimes as a rarity we had a little bread, which was made of Indian corn meal, pounded in a homony-block, mixed with boiled beans, and baked in cakes under the ashes.

This, with us was called good living, though not equal to our fat, roasted and boiled venison, when we went to the woods in the fall; or bears meat and beaver in the winter; or sugar, bears oil, and dry venison in the spring.

Some time in October, another adopted brother, older than Tontileaugo, came to pay us a visit at Sunyendeand, and he asked me to take a hunt with him on Cayahaga. As they always used me as a free man, and gave me the liberty of choosing, I told him that I was attached to Tontileaugo—had never seen him before, and therefore, asked sometime to consider of this. He told me that the party he was going with would not be along, or at the mouth of this little lake, in less than six days, and I could in this time be acquainted with him, and judge for myself. I consulted with Tontileaugo on this occasion, and he told me that our older brother Tecaughretanego, (which was his name) was a chief, and a better man than he was; and if I might do as I pleased; and if I staid he would use me as he had done. I told him that he had acted in every respect, as a brother to me; yet I was much pleased with my old brother's conduct and conversation; and as he was going to a part of the country I had never been in, I wished to go with him—he said that he was perfectly willing.

I then went with Tecaughretanego, to the mouth of the little lake, where he met with the company he intended going with, which was composed of, Caughnewagas, and Ottawas. Here I was introduced to a Caughnewaga sister, and others I had never before seen. My sister's name was Mary, which they pronounced *Maully.* I asked Tecaughretanego how it came that she had an English name; he said that he did not know that it was an English name; but it was the name the priest gave her when she was baptized, which he said was the name of the mother of Jesus. He said there were a great many of the Caughnewagas and Wiandots, that were a kind of half Roman-Catholics; but as for himself, he said, that the priest and him could not agree; as they held notions that contradicted both sense and reason, and had the assurance to tell him, that the book of God, taught them these foolish absurdities: but he could not believe the great and good spirit ever taught them any such nonsense: and therefore he concluded that the Indians' old religion was better than this new way of worshiping God.

The Ottawas have a very useful kind of tents which they carry with them, made of flags, plaited and stitched together in a very artful manner, so as to turn rain, or wind well—each mat is made fifteen feet long, and about five feet broad. In order to erect this kind of tent, they cut a number of long strait poles, which they drive in the ground, in form of a circle, leaning inwards; then they spread the matts on these poles—beginning at the bottom and extending up, leaving only a hole in the top uncovered—and this hole answers the place of a chimney. They make a fire of dry split wood, in the middle, and spread down bark mats and skins for bedding, on which they sleep in a crooked posture, all round the fire, as the length of their beds will not admit of stretching themselves. In place of a door they lift up one end of a mat and creep in, and let the mat fall down behind them.

These tents are warm and dry, and tolerable clear of smoke. Their lumber they keep under birch-bark canoes, which they carry out and turn up for a shelter, where they keep every thing from the rain. Nothing is in the tents but themselves and their bedding.

This company had four birch canoes and four tents. We were kindly received, and they gave us plenty of homony, and wild fowl, boiled and roasted. As the geese, ducks, swans, &c. here are well grain-fed, they were remarkably fat especially the green necked ducks.

The wild fowl here, feed upon a kind of wild rice, that grows spontaneously in the shallow water, or wet places along the sides or in the corners of the lakes.

As the wind was high and we could not proceed on our voyage, we remained here several days, and killed abundance of wild fowl, and a number of racoons.

When a company of Indians are moving together on the lake, as it is at this time of the year often dangerous sailing, the old men hold a council; and when they agree to embark, every one is engaged immediately in making ready, without offering one word against the measure, though the lake may be boisterous and horrid. One morning tho' the wind appeared to me to be as high as in days past, and the billows raging, yet the call was given *yohoh-yohoh*, which was quickly answered by all – *ooh-ooh* which signifies agreed. We were all instantly engaged in preparing to start, and had considerable difficulties in embarking.

As soon as we got into our canoes we fell to paddling with all our might, making out from the shore. Though these sort of canoes ride waves beyond what could be expected, yet the water several times dashed into them. When we got out about half a mile from shore, we hoisted sail, and as it was nearly a west wind, we then seemed to ride the waves with ease, and went on at a rapid rate. We then all laid down our paddles, excepting one that steered, and there was no water dashed into our canoes, until we came near the shore again. We sailed about sixty miles that day, and encamped some time before night.

The next day we again embarked and went on very well for some time; but the lake being boisterous, and the wind not fair, we were obliged to make to shore, which we accomplished with hard work and some difficulty in landing. – The next morning a council was held by the old men.

As we had this day to pass by a long precipice of rocks, on the shore about nine miles, which rendered it impossible for us to land, though the wind was high and the lake rough; yet, as it was fair, we were all ordered to embark. We wrought ourselves out from the shore and hoisted sail (what we used in place of sail cloth, were our tent mats, which answered the place very well) and went on for some time with a fair wind, until we were opposite to the precipice, and then it turned towards the shore, and we began to fear we should be cast upon the rocks. Two of the canoes were considerably farther out from the rocks, than the canoe I was in. Those who were farthest out in the lake did not let down their sails until they had passed the precipice; but as we were nearer the rock, we were obliged to lower our sails, and paddle with all our might. With much difficulty we cleared ourselves of the rock, and landed. As the other canoes had landed before us, there were immediately runners sent off to see if we were all safely landed.

This night the wind fell, and the next morning the lake was tolerably calm, and we embarked without difficulty, and paddled along near the shore, until we came to the mouth of Cayahaga, which empties into Lake Erie on the south side, betwixt Canesadooharie, and Presq'Isle.

We turned up Cayahaga and encamped—where we staid and hunted for several days; and so we kept moving and hunting until we came to the forks of Cayahaga.

This is a very gentle river, and but few riffles, or swift running places, from the mouth to the forks. Deer here were tolerably plenty, large and fat; but bear and other game scarce. The upland is hilly, and principally second and third rate land. The timber chiefly black-oak, white-oak, hickory, dogwood &c. The bottoms are rich and large, and the timber is walnut, locust, mulberry, sugar-tree, red-haw, black-haw, wild-appletrees &c. The West Branch of this river interlocks with the East Branch of Muskingum; and the East Branch with the Big Beaver creek, that empties into the Ohio about thirty miles below Pittsburgh.

From the forks of Cayahaga to the East Branch of Muskingum, there is a carrying place, where the Indians carry their canoes &c. from the waters of Lake Erie, into the waters of the Ohio.

From the forks I went over with some hunters, to the East Branch of Muskingum, where they killed several deer, a number of beavers, and returned heavy laden, with skins and meat, which we carried on our backs, as we had no horses.

The land here is chiefly second and third rate, and the timber chiefly oak and hickory. A little above the forks, on the East Branch of Cayahaga, are considerable rapids, very rocky, for some distance; but no perpendicular falls.

About the first of December, 1756, we were preparing for leaving the river: we buried our canoes, and as usual hung up our skins, and every one had a pack to carry: the squaws also packed up their tents, which they carried in large rolls, that extended up above their heads; and though a great bulk, yet not heavy. We steered about a south east course and could not march over ten miles per day. At night we lodged in our flag tents, which when erected, were nearly in the shape of a sugar loaf, and about fifteen feet diameter at the ground.

In this manner we proceeded about forty miles, and wintered in these tents, on the waters of Beaver creek, near a little lake or large pond, which is about two miles long, and one broad, and a remarkable place for beaver.

It is a received opinion among the Indians, that the geese turn to beavers, and the snakes to racoons; and though Tecaughretanego, who was a wise man, was not fully persuaded that this was true; yet he seemed in some measure to be carried away with this whimsical notion. He said that this pond had been always a plentiful place of beaver. Though he said he knew them to be frequently all killed, (as he thought;) yet the next winter they would be as plenty as ever. And as the beaver was an animal that did not travel by land, and there being no water communication, to, or from this pond—how could such a number of beavers get there year after year? But as this pond was also a considerable place for geese, when they came in the fall from the north, and alighted in this pond, they turned beavers, all but the feet, which remained nearly the same.

I said, that though there was no water communication, in, or out of this pond; yet it appeared that it was fed by springs, as it was always clear and never stagnated: and as a very large spring rose about a mile below this pond, it was likely that this spring came from this pond. In the fall when this spring is comparatively low there would be air under ground sufficient for the beavers to breathe in, with their heads above water, for they cannot live long under water, and so they might have a subterraneous passage by water into this pond. —Tecaughretanego, granted that it might be so.

About the tides of this pond there grew great abundance of cranberries, which the Indians gathered up on the ice, when the pond was frozen over. These berries were about as large as rifle bullets—of a bright red color—an agreeable sour, though rather too sour of themselves; but when mixed with sugar, had a very agreeable taste.

In conversation with Tecaughretanego, I happened to be talking of the beavers' catching fish. He asked me why I thought that the beaver caught fish? I told him that I had read of the beaver making dams for the conveniency of fishing. He laughed and made game of me and my book. He said the man that wrote that book knew nothing about the beaver. The beaver never did eat flesh of any kind; but lived on the bark of trees, roots, and other vegetables.

In order to know certainly how this was, when we killed a beaver I carefully examined the intestines but found no appearance of fish; I afterwards made an experiment on a pet beaver which we had, and found that it would neither eat fish or flesh; therefore I acknowledged that the book I had read was wrong.

I asked him if the beaver was an amphibious animal, or if it could live under water? He said that the beaver was a kind of subterraneous water animal, that lives in or near the water; but they were no more amphibious than the ducks and geese were—which was constantly proven to be the case; as all the beavers that are caught in steel traps are drowned, provided the trap be heavy enough to keep them under water. As the beaver does not eat fish, I enquired of Tecaughretanego why the beaver made such large dams? He said they were of use to them in various respects—both for their safety and food. For their safety, as by raising the water over the mouths of their holes; or subterraneous lodging places, they could not be easily found: and as the beaver feeds chiefly on the bark of trees, by raising the water over the banks, they can cut down saplings for bark to feed upon without going out much upon the land: and when they are obliged to go out on land for this food they frequently are caught by the wolves. As the beaver can run upon land, but little faster than a water tortoise, and is no fighting animal, if they are any distance from the water they become an easy prey to their enemies.

I asked Tecaughretanego, what was the use of the beaver's stones, or glands, to them; – as the beaver has two pair, which is commonly called the oil stones, and the bark stones? He said that as the beavers are the dumbest of all animals, and scarcely ever make any noise; and as they were working creatures, they made use of this smell in order to work in concert. If an old beaver was to come on the bank and rub his breech upon the ground, and raise a perfume, the others will collect from different places and go to work: this is also of use to them in travelling, that they may thereby search out and find their company. Cunning hunters finding this out, have made use of it against the beaver, in order to catch them. What is the bait which you see them make use of, but a compound of the oil and bark stones? By this perfume, which is only a false signal, they decoy them to the trap.

Near this pond, beaver was the principal game. Before the waters froze up, we caught a great many with wooden and steel traps: but after that, we hunted the beaver on the ice. Some places here the beavers build large houses to live in; and, in other places they have subterraneous lodgings in the banks. Where they lodge in the ground we have no chance of hunting them on the ice; but where they have houses, we go with malls and handspikes, and break all the hollow ice to prevent them from getting their heads above the water under it. Then we break a hole in the house and they make their escape into the water; but as they cannot live long under water, they are obliged to go to some of those broken places to breathe, and the Indians commonly put in their hands, catch them by the hind leg, hawl them on the ice, and tomahawk them. Sometimes they shoot them in the head, when they raise it above the water. I asked the Indians if they were not afraid to catch the beavers with their hands? They said no: they were not much of a biting creature; yet if they would catch them by the fore foot, they would bite.

I went out with Tecaughretanego, and some others a beaver hunting: but we did not succeed, and on our return we saw where several racoons had passed, while the snow was soft; tho' there was now a crust upon it, we all made a halt looking at the racoon tracks. As they saw a tree with a hole in it they told me to go and see if they had gone in thereat; and if they had, to *halloo*, and they would come and take them out. When I went to that tree, I found they had gone past; but I saw another the way they had went, and proceeded to examine that, and found they had gone up it. I then began to *halloo*, but could have no answer.

As it began to snow and blow most violently, I returned and proceeded after my company, and for some time could see their tracks; but the old snow being only about three inches deep, and a crust upon it, the present driving snow soon filled up the tracks. As I had only a bow, arrows and tomahawk with me, and no way to strike fire, I appeared to be in a dismal situation—and as the air was dark with snow, I had little more prospect of steering my course, than I would in the night. At length I came to a hollow tree, with a hole at one side that I could go in at. I went in, and found that it was a dry place, and the hollow about three feet diameter, and high enough for me to stand in. I found that there was also a considerable quantity of soft, dry rotten wood, around this hollow: I therefore concluded that I would lodge here; and that I would go to work, and stop up the door of my house. I stripped off my blanket, (which was all the clothes that I had, excepting a breech-clout, leggings and mockasons), and with my tomahawk, fell to chopping at the top of a fallen tree that lay near and carried wood and set it up on end against the door, until I had it three or four feet thick, all round, excepting a hole I had left to creep in at. I had a block prepared that I could hawl after me, to stop this hole: and before I went in I put in a number of small sticks, that I might more effectually stop it on the inside. When I went in, I took my tomahawk and cut down all the dry rotten wood I could get, and beat it small. With it I made a bed like a goose-nest or hog-bed, and with the small sticks stopped every hole, until my house was almost dark. I stripped off my mockasons, and danced in the centre of my bed for about half an hour, in order to warm myself. In this time my feet and whole body were agreeable warmed. The snow, in the mean while, had stopped all the holes, so that my house was as dark as a dungeon; though I knew it could not yet be dark out of doors. I then coiled myself up in my blanket, lay down in my little round bed, and had a tolerable nights lodging. When I awoke, all was dark—not the least glimmering of light was to be seen. Immediately I recollected that I was not to expect light in this new habitation, as there was neither door nor window in it. As I could hear the storm raging, and did not suffer much cold, as I was then situated, I concluded I would stay in my nest until I was certain it was day. When I had reason to conclude that it surely was day, I arose and put on my mockasons, which I had laid under my head to keep from freezing. I then endeavored to find the door, and had to do all by the sense of feeling, which took me some time. At length I found the block, but it being heavy, and a large quantity of snow having fallen on it, at the first attempt I did not move it. I then felt terrified—among all the hardships I had sustained, I never knew before, what it was to be thus deprived of light. This, with the other circumstances attending it, appeared grievous. I went straightway to bed again, wrapped my blanket round me, and lay and mused awhile, and then prayed to

Almighty God to direct and protect me, as He had done heretofore. I once again attempted to move away the block, which proved successful: it moved about nine inches. With this a considerable quantity of snow fell in from above, and I immediately received light; so that I found a very great snow had fallen, above what I had ever seen in one night. I then knew why I could not easily move the block, and I was so rejoiced at obtaining the light, that all my other difficulties seemed to vanish. I then turned into my cell, and returned God thanks for having once more received the light of Heaven. At length I belted my blanket about me, got my tomahawk, bow and arrows, and went out of my den.

I was now in tolerable high spirits, tho' the snow had fallen above three feet deep, in addition to what was on the ground before; and the only imperfect guide I had, in order to steer my course to camp, was the trees; as the moss generally grows on the north-west side of the, if they are straight. I proceeded on, wading through the snow, and about twelve o'clock (as it appeared afterwards, from that time to night, for it was yet cloudy), I came upon the creek that our camp was on about half a mile below the camp; and when I came in sight of the camp, I found that there was great joy, by the shouts and yelling of the boys, &c.

When I arrived, they all came round me, and received me gladly; but at this time no questions were asked, and I was taken into a tent, where they gave me plenty of fat beaver meat, and then asked me to smoke. When I had done, Tecaughretanego desired me to walk out to a fire they had made. I went out, and they all collected round me, both men, women and boys. Tecaughretanego asked me to give them a particular account of what had happened from the time they left me yesterday, until now. I told them the whole of the story, and they never interrupted me; but when I made a stop, the intervals were filled with loud acclamations of joy. As I could not, at this time, talk Ottawa or Jibewa well, (which is nearly the same) I delivered my story in Caughnewaga. As my sister Molly's husband was a Jibewa and could understand Caughnewaga, he acted as interpreter, and delivered my story to the Jibewas and Ottawas, which they received with pleasure. When all this was done, Tecaughretanego made a speech to me in the following manner:

"Brother,

"You see we have prepared snow-shoes to go after you, and were almost ready to go, when you appeared; yet, as you had not been accustomed to hardships in your country, to the east, we never expected to see you alive. Now, we are glad to see you, in various respects: we are glad to see you on your own account; and we are glad to see the prospect of your filling the place of a great man, in whose room you were adopted. We do not blame you for what has happened, we blame ourselves; because, we did not think of this driving snow filling up the tracks, until after we came to camp."

"Brother,

"Your conduct on this occasion hath pleased us much: You have given us an evidence of your fortitude, skill and resolution: and we hope you will always go on to do great actions, as it is only great actions that can make a great man."

I told my brother Tecaughretanego, that I thanked them for their care of me, and for the kindness I always received. I told him that I always wished to do great actions, and hoped I never would do any thing to dishonor any of those with whom I was connected. I likewise told my Jibewa brother-in-law to tell his people that I also thanked them for their care and kindness.

The next morning some of the hunters went out on snow-shoes, killed several deer, and hauled some of them into camp upon the snow. They fixed their carrying strings, (which are broad in the middle, and small at each end) in the fore feet and nose of the deer, and laid the broad part of it on their heads or about their shoulders, and pulled it along; and when it is moving, will not sink in the snow much deeper than a snow-shoe; and when taken with the grain of the hair, slips along very easy.

The snow-shoes are made like a hoop net, and wrought with buck-skin thongs. Each shoe is about two feet and an half long, and about eighteen inches broad, before, and small behind, with cross bars, in order to fix or tie them to their feet. After the snow had lay a few days, the Indians tomahawked the deer, by pursuing them in this manner.

About two weeks after this, there came a warm rain, and took away the chief part of the snow, and broke up the ice: then we engaged in making wooden traps to catch beavers, as we had but few steel traps. These traps are made nearly in the same manner as the racoon traps already described.

One day as I was looking after my traps, I got benighted, by beaver ponds intercepting my way to camp; and as I had neglected to take fire-works with me, and the weather very cold, I could find no suitable lodging place, therefore the only expedient I could think of to keep myself from freezing, was exercise. I danced and halloo'd the whole night with all my might, and the next day came to camp. Though I suffered much more this time than the other night I lay out, yet the

Indians were not so much concerned, as they thought I had fire-works with me; but when they knew how it was, they did not blame me. They said that old hunters were frequently involved in this place, as the beaver dams were one above another on every creek and run, so that it is hard to find a fording place. The applauded me for my fortitude, and said as they had now plenty of beaver-skins, they would purchase me a new gun at Detroit, as we were to go there the next spring; and then if I should chance to be lost in dark weather, I could make fire, kill provision, and return to camp when the sun shined. By being bewildered on the waters of Muskingum, I lost repute, and was reduced to the bow and arrow; and by lying out two nights here, I regained my credit.

After some time the waters all froze again, and then, as formerly, we hunted beavers on the ice. Though beaver meat, without salt or bread, was the chief of our food this winter, yet we had always plenty, and I was well contented with my diet, as it appeared delicious fare, after the way we had lived the winter before.

Sometime in February, we scaffolded up our fur and skins, and moved about ten miles in quest of a sugar camp, or a suitable place to make sugar, and encamped in a large bottom, on the head waters of Big Beaver creek. We had some difficulty in moving, as we had a blind Caughnewaga boy about 15 years of age, to lead; and as this country is very brushy, we frequently had him to carry; We had also my Jibewa brother-in-law's father with us, who was thought by the Indians to be a great conjuror—his name was Manetohcoa—this old man was so decrepit, that we had to carry him this route upon a bier, and all our baggage to pack on our backs.

Shortly after we came to this place the squaws began to make sugar. We had no large kettles with us this year, and they made the frost, in some measure, supply the place of fire, in making sugar. Their large bark vessels, for holding the stock-water, they made broad and shallow; and as the weather is very cold here, it frequently freezes at night in sugar time; and the ice they break and cast out of the vessels. I asked them if they were not throwing away the sugar? they said no: it was water they were casting away, sugar did not freeze, and there was scarcely any in that ice. They said I might try the experiment, and boil some of it, and see what I would get. I never did try it; but I observed that after several times freezing, the water that remained in the vessel, changed its color and became brown and very sweet.

About the time we were done making sugar the snow went off the ground; and one night a squaw raised an alarm. She said she saw two men with guns in their hands, upon the bank on the other side of the creek, spying our tents—they were supposed to be Johnston's Mohawks. On this the squaws were ordered to slip quietly out, some distance into the bushes; and all who had either guns or bows were to squat in the bushes near the tents; and if the enemy rushed up, we were to give them the first fire, and let the squaws have an opportunity of escaping. I got down beside Tecaughretanego, and he whispered to me not to be afraid, for he would speak to the Mohawks, and as they spake the same tongue that we did, they would not hurt the Caughnewagas, or me: but they would kill all the Jibewas and Ottawas that they could, and take us along with them. The news pleased me well, and I heartily wished for the approach of the Mohawks.

Before we withdrew from the tents they had carried Manetohcoa to the fire, and gave him his conjuring tools; which were dyed feathers, the bone of the shoulder blade of a wild cat, tobacco &c. and while we were in the bushes, Manetohcoa was in a tent at the fire, conjuring away to the utmost of his ability. At length he called aloud for us all to come in, which was quickly obeyed. When we came in, he told us that after he had gone through the whole of his ceremony, and expected to see a number of Mohawks on the flat bone when it was warmed at the fire, the pictures of two wolves only appeared. He said tho there were no Mohawks about, we must not be angry with the squaw for giving a false alarm; as she had occasion to go out and happened to see the wolves, though it was moon light; yet she got afraid, and she conceited it was Indians, with guns in their hands, so he said we might all go to sleep for there was no danger—and accordingly we did.

The next morning we went to the place, and found wolf tracks, and where they had scratched with their feet like dogs; but there was no sign of mockason tracks. If there is any such thing as a wizzard, I think Manetohcoa was as likely to be one, as any man, as he was a professed worshiper of the devil. –But let him be a conjuror or not, I am persuaded that the Indians believed what he told them upon this occasion, as well as if it had come from an infallible oracle; or they would not after such an alarm as this, go all to sleep in an unconcerned manner. This appeared to me the most like witchcraft, of anything I beheld while I was with them. Though I scrutinized their proceedings in business of this kind; yet I generally found that their pretended witchcraft, was either art or mistaken notions whereby they deceived themselves. Before a battle, they spy the enemy's motions carefully, and when they find that they can have considerable advantage, and the greatest prospect of success, then the old men pretend to conjure, or to tell what the event will be, --and this they do in a figurative manner, which will bear something of a different interpretation, which generally comes to pass nearly as they foretold; therefore the young warriors generally believed these old conjurors, which had a tendency to animate, and excite them to push on with vigor.

Some time in March 1757 we began to move back to the forks of Cayahaga, which was about forty or fifty miles; and as we had no horses, we had all our baggage and several hundred weight of beaver skins, and some deer and bear skins—all to pack on our backs. The method we took to accomplish this was by making short day's journies. In the morning we would move on with as much as we were able to carry, about five miles, and encamp; and then run back for more. We commonly made three such trips in the day. When we came to the great pond, we staid there one day to rest ourselves and to kill ducks and geese.

While we remained here I went in company with a young Caughnewaga, who was about sixteen or seventeen years of age, Chinnohete by name, in order to gather crannberries. As he was gathering berries at some distance from me, three Jibewa squaws crept up undiscovered and made at him speedily, but he nimbly escaped and came to me apparently terrified. I asked him what he was afraid of? He replied did you not see those squaws? I told him I did, and they appeared to be in a very good humour. I asked him wherefore then he was afraid of them? He said the Jibewa squaws were very bad women, and had a very ugly custom among them. I asked him what that custom was? He said that when two or three of them could catch a young lad, that was betwixt a man and a boy, out by himself, if they could overpower him, they would strip him by force in order to see whether he was coming on to be a man or not. He said that was what they intended when they crawled up, and ran so violently at him, but said he, I am very glad that I so narrowly escaped. I then agreed with Chinnohete in condemning this as a bad custom, and an exceeding immodest action for young women to be guilty of.

From our sugar camp on the head waters of Big Beaver creek, to this place is not hilly, and some places the woods are tolerably clear; but in most places exceeding brushy. The land here is chiefly second and third rate. The timber on the upland is white-oak, black-oak, hickory and chesnut: there is also in some places walnut up land, and plenty of good water. The bottoms here are generally large and good.

We again proceeded on from the pond to the forks of Cayahaga, at the rate of about five miles per day.

The land on this route is not very hilly, it is well watered, and in many places ill timbered, generally brushy, and chiefly second and third rate land, intermixed with good bottoms.

When we came to the forks, we found that the skins we had scaffolded were all safe. Though this was a public place, and Indians frequently passing, and our skins hanging up in view; yet there was none stolen, and it is seldom that Indians do steal any thing from one another; and they say they never did, until the white people came among them, and learned some of them, to lie, cheat and steal, --but be that as it may, they never did curse or swear, until the whites learned them; some think their language will not admit of it, but I am not of that opinion, if I was so disposed, I could find language to curse or swear, in the Indian tongue.

I remember that Tecaughretanego, when something displeased him, said, God damn it. --I asked him if he knew what he then said? He said he did; and mentioned one of their degrading expressions, which he supposed to be the meaning or something like the meaning of what he had said. I told him that it did not bear the least resemblance to it; that what he said, was calling upon the great spirit to punish the object he was displeased with. He stood for sometime amazed, and then said, if this be the meaning of these words what sort of people are the whites? When the traders were among us these words seemed to be intermixed with all their discourse. He told me to reconsider what I had said, for he thought I must be mistaken in my definition; if I was not mistaken, he said, the traders applied these words not only wickedly, but often times very foolishly and contrary to sense or reason. He said he remembered once of a trader's accidentally breaking his gun lock, and on that occasion calling out loud God damn it—surely said he the gun lock was not an object worthy of punishment for Owaneeyo, or the Great Spirit: he also observed the traders often used this expression, when they were in a good humour and not displeased with any thing. --I acknowledged that the traders used this expression very often, in a most irrational, inconsistent, and impious manner; yet I still asserted that I had given the true meaning of these words. --He replied, if so, the traders are as bad as Oonasahroona, or the under ground inhabitants, which is the name they give the devils; as they entertain a notion that their place of residence is under the earth.

We took up our birch-bark canoes which we had buried, and found that they were not damaged by the winter; but they not being sufficient to carry all that we now had, we made a large chesnut bark canoe, as elm bark was not to be found at this place.

We all embarked, and had a very agreeable passage down the Cayahaga, and along the south side of Lake Erie, until we passed the mouth of Sandusky; then the wind arose, and we put in at the mouth of the Miami of the Lake, at Cedar Point, where we remained several days, and killed a number of turkeys, geese, ducks and swans. The wind being fair, and the lake not extremely rough, we again embarked, hoisted up sails, and arrived safe at the Wiandot town, nearly opposite to Fort Detroit, on the north side of the river. Here we found a number of French traders, every one very willing to deal with us for our beaver.

We bought ourselves fine clothes, amunition, paint, tobacco, &c. and according to promise, they purchased me a new gun: yet we had parted with only about one third of our beaver. At length a trader came to town with French Brandy: we purchased a keg of it, and held a council about who was to get drunk, and who was to keep sober. I was invited to get drunk, but I refused the proposal—then they told me that I must be one of those who were to take care of the drunken people. I did not like this; but of two evils I chose that which I thought was the least—and fell in with those who were to conceal the arms, and keep every dangerous weapon we could, out of their way, and endeavor, if possible to keep the drinking club from killing each other, which was a very hard task. Several times we hazarded our own lives, and got ourselves hurt, in preventing them from slaying each other. Before they had finished this keg, near one third of the town was introduced to this drinking club; they could not pay their part, as they had already disposed of all their skins; but that made no odds, all were welcome to drink.

When they were done with this keg, they applied to the traders, and procured a kettle full of brandy at a time, which they divided out with a large wooden spoon,--and so they went on and never quit while they had a single beaver skin.

When the trader had got all our beaver, he moved off to the Ottawa town, about a mile above the Wiandot town.

When the brandy was gone, and the drinking club sober, they appeared much dejected. Some of them were crippled, others badly wounded, a number of their fine new shirts tore, and several blankets were burned:--a number of squaws were also in this club and neglected their corn planting.

We could now hear the effects of the brandy in the Ottawa town. They were singing and yelling in the most hideous manner, both night and day; but their frolic ended worse than ours; five Ottawas were killed and a great many wounded.

After this a number of young Indians were getting their ears cut, and they urged me to have mine cut likewise; but they did not attempt to compel me, though they endeavoured to persuade me. The principal arguments they used were its being a very great ornament, and also the common fashion – The former I did not believe, and the latter I could not deny. The way they performed this operation was by cutting the fleshy part of the circle of the ear close to the gristle quite through. When this was done they wrapt rags round this fleshy part until it was entirely healed; then they hung lead to it and stretched it to a wonderful length: when it was sufficiently stretched, they wrapt the fleshy part round with brass wire, which formed it into a semicircle about four inches diameter.

Many of the young men were now exercising themselves in a game resembling foot ball; though they commonly struck the ball with a crooked stick, made for the purpose; also a game something like this, wherein they used a wooden ball, about three inches diameter, and the instrument they moved it with was a strong staff about five feet long, with a hoop net on the end of it, large enough to contain the ball. Before they begin the play, they lay off about half a mile distance in a clear plain, and the opposite parties all attend at the centre, where a disinterested person casts up the ball then the opposite parties all contend for it. If any one gets it into his net, he runs with it the way he wishes it to go, and they all pursue him. If one of the opposite party overtakes the person with the ball, he gives the staff a stroke which causes the ball to fly out of the net; then they have another debate for it; and if the one that gets it can outrun all the opposite party, and can carry it quite out, or over the line at the end, the game is won; but this seldom happens. When any one is running away with the ball, and is like to be overtaken, he commonly throws it, and with this instrument can cast it fifty or sixty yards. Sometimes when the ball is almost at the one end, matters will take a sudden turn, and the opposite party may quickly carry it out at the other end. Often times they will work a long while back and forward before they can get the ball over the line, or win the game.

About the first of June 1757 the warriors were preparing to go to war, in the Wiandot, Pottowatomy, and Ottawa towns; also a great many Jibewas came down from the upper lakes; and after singing their war songs and going through their common ceremonies, they marched off against the frontiers of Virginia, Maryland and Pennsylvania, in their usual manner, singing the travelling song, slow firing, &c.

On the north side of the river St. Laurence, opposite to Fort Detroit, there is an island, which the Indians call the Long Island, and which they say is above one thousand miles long, and in some places above one hundred miles broad. They further say that the great river that comes down by Canesatauga and that empties into the main branch of St. Laurence, above Montreal, originates from one source, with the St. Lawrence, and forms this island.

Opposite to Detroit, and below it, was originally a prairie, and laid off in lots about sixty rods broad, and a great length; each lot is divided into two fields, which they cultivate year about. The principal grain that the French raised in these fields was spring wheat, and peas.

They built all their houses on the front of these lots on the river side; and as the banks of the river are very low, some of the houses are not above three or four feet above the surface of the water; yet they are in no danger of being disturbed by freshes, as the river seldom rises above eighteen inches; because it is the communication, of the river St. Laurence, from one lake to another.

As dwelling houses, barns, and stables are all built on the front of these lots; at a distance it appears like a continued row of houses in a town, on each side of the river for a long way. These villages, the town, the river and the plains, being all in view at once, affords a most delightful prospect.

The inhabitants here chiefly drink the river water; and as it comes from the northward it is very wholesome.

The land here is principally second rate, and comparatively speaking, a small part is first or third rate; tho about four or five miles south of Detroit, their is a small portion that is worse than what I would call the third rate, which produces abundance of hurtle berries.

There is plenty of good meadow ground here, and a great many marshes that are overspread with water. –The timber is elm, sugar-tree, black-ash, white-ash, abundance of water-ash, oak, hickory, and some walnut.

About the middle of June the Indians were almost all gone to war, from sixteen to sixty; yet Tecaughretanego remained in town with me. Tho he had formerly, when they were at war with the southern nations been a great warrior, and an eminent counsellor; and I think as clear and as able a reasoner upon any subject that he had an opportunity of being acquainted with, as I ever knew; yet he had all along been against this war, and had strenuously opposed it in council. He said if the English and French had a quarrel let them fight their own battles themselves; it is not our business to intermeddle therewith.

Before the warriors returned we were very bare of provision: and tho we did not commonly steal from one another; yet we stole during this time any thing that we could eat from the French, under the notion that it was just for us to do so; because they supported their soldiers; and our squaws, old men and children were suffering on the account of the war, as our hunters were all gone.

Some time in August the warriors returned, and brought in with them a great many scalps, prisoners, horses and plunder; and the common report among the young warriors, was, that they would intirely subdue Tulhasaga, that is the English, or it might be literally rendered the Morning Light inhabitants.

About the first of November a number of families were preparing to go on their winter hunt, and all agreed to cross the lake together. We encamped at the mouth of the river the first night, and a council was held, whether we would cross thro' by the three islands, or coast it round the lake. These islands lie in a line across the lake, and are just in sight of each other. Some of the Wiandots or Ottawa frequently make their winter hunt on these islands. Tho excepting wild fowl and fish, there is scarcely any game here but racoons which are amazingly plenty, and exceeding large and fat; as they feed upon the wild rice, which grows in abundance in wet places round these islands. It is said that each hunter in one winter will catch one thousand racoons.

It is a received opinion among the Indians that the snakes and racoons are transmutable; and that a great many of the snakes turn racoons every fall, and racoons snakes every spring. This notion is founded on observations made on the snakes and racoons in this island.

As the racoons here lodge in rocks, the trappers make their wooden traps at the mouth of the holes; and as they go daily to look at their traps, in the winter season, they commonly find them filled with racoons; but in the spring or when the frost is out of the ground, they say, they then find their traps filled with large rattle snakes. And therefore conclude that the racoons are transformed. They also say that the reason why they are so remarkably plenty in the winter, is every fall the snakes turn racoons again.

I told them that tho I had never landed on any of these islands, yet from the unanimous accounts I had received I believed that both snakes and racoons were plenty there; but no doubt they all remained there both summer and winter, only the snakes were not to be seen in the latter; yet I did not believe that they were transmutable.

These islands are but seldom visited; because early in the spring and late in the fall it is dangerous sailing in their bark canoes; and in the summer they are so infested with various kinds of serpents, (but chiefly rattle snakes,) that it is dangerous landing.

I shall now quit this digression, and return to the result of the council at the mouth of the river. We concluded to coast it round the lake, and in two days we came to the mouth of the Miami of the Lake, and landed on cedar point, where we remained several days. Here we held a council, and concluded we would take a driving hunt in concert, and in partnership.

The river in this place is about a mile broad, and as it and the lake forms a kind of neck, which terminates in a point, all the hunters (which were fifty-three) went up the river, and we scattered ourselves from the river to the lake. When we first began to move we were not in sight of each other, but as we all raised the yell, we could move regularly together by the noise. At length we came in sight of each other and appeared to be marching in good order; before we came to the point, both the squaws and boys in the canoes were scattered up the river, and along the lake, to prevent the deer from making their escape by water. As we advanced near the point the guns began to crack slowly; and after some time the firing was like a little engagement. The squaws and boys were busy tomahawking the deer in the water, and we shooting them down on the land: -- We killed in all about thirty deer: tho a great many made their escape by water.

We had now great feasting and rejoicing, as we had plenty of homony, venison, and wild fowl. The geese at this time appeared to be preparing to move southward—It might be asked what is meant by the geese preparing to move? The Indians represent them as holding a great council at this time concerning the weather in order to conclude upon a day, that they may all at or near one time leave the Northern Lakes, and wing their way to the southern bays. When matters are brought to a conclusion and the time appointed that they are to take wing, then they say, a great number of expresses are sent off, in order to let the different tribes know the result of this council, that they may be all in readiness to move at the time appointed. As there is a great commotion among the geese at this time, it would appear by their actions, that such a council had been held. Certain it is, that they are led by instinct to act in concert and to move off regularly after their leaders.

Here our company separated. The chief part of them went up the Miami river, that empties into Lake Erie, at cedar point, whilst we proceeded on our journey in company with Tecaughretanego, Tontileaugo, and two families of the Wiandots.

As cold weather was now approaching, we began to feel the doleful effects of extravagantly and foolishly spending the large quantity of beaver we had taken in our last winters hunt. We were all nearly in the same circumstances—scarcely one had a shirt to his back; but each of us had an old blanket which we belted round us in the day, and slept in at night, with a deer or bear skin under us for our bed.

When we came to the falls of Sandusky, we buried our birch bark canoes as usual, at a large burying place for that purpose, a little below the falls. At this place the river falls about eight feet over a rock, but not perpendicular. With much difficulty we pushed up our wooden canoes, some of us went up the river, and the rest by land with the horses, until we came to the great meadows or prairies that lie between Sandusky and Sciota.

When we came to this place we met with some Ottawa hunters, and agreed with them to take, what they call a ring hunt, in partnership. We waited until we expected rain was near falling to extinguish the fire, and then we kindled a large circle in the prairie. At this time, or before the bucks began to run a great number of deer lay concealed in the grass, in the day, and moved about in the night; but as the fire burned in towards the centre of the circle, the deer fled before the fire: the Indians were scattered also at some distance before the fire, and shot them down every opportunity, which was very frequent, especially as the circle became small. When we came to divide the deer, there were above ten to each hunter, which were all killed in a few hours. The rain did not come on that night to put out the out-side circle of the fire, and as the wind arose, it extended thro the whole prairie which was about fifty miles in length, and in some places near twenty in breadth. This put an end to our ring hunting this season, and was in other respects an injury to us in the hunting business; so that upon the whole we received more harm than benefit by our rapid hunting frolic. We then moved from the north end of the glades, and encamped at the carrying place.

This place is in the plains betwixt a creek that empties into Sandusky, and one that runs into Scotia: and at the time of high water, or in the spring season, there is but about one half mile of portage, and that very level, and clear of rocks, timber or stones; so that with a little digging there may be water carriage the whole way from Scotia to Lake Erie.

From the mouth of Sandusky to the falls is chiefly first rate land, lying flat or level, intermixed with large bodies of clear meadows, where the grass is exceeding rank, and in many places three or four feet high. The timber is oak, hickory, walnut, cherry, black-ash, elm, sugar-tree, buckeye, locust and beech. In some places there is wet timber land—the timber in these places is chiefly water-ash, sycamore, or button-wood.

From the falls to the prairies, the land lies well to the sun, it is neither too flat nor too hilly—and chiefly first rate. The timber nearly the same as below the falls, excepting the water-ash.—There is also here, some plats of beech land, that appears to be second rate, as it frequently produces spice-wood. The prairie appears to be a tolerable fertile soil, tho in many places too wet for cultivation; yet I apprehend it would produce timber, were it only kept from fire.

The Indians are of the opinion that the squirrels plant all the timber; as they bury a number of nuts for food, and only one at a place. When a squirrel is killed the various kinds of nuts thus buried will grow.

I have observed that when these prairies have only escaped fire for one year, near where a single tree stood, there was a young growth of timber supposed to be planted by the squirrels; but when the prairies were again burned, all this young growth was immediately consumed; as the fire rages in the grass, to such a pitch, that numbers of racoons are thereby burned to death.

On the west side of the prairie, or betwixt that and Sciota, there is a large body of first rate land—the timber, walnut, locust, sugar-tree, buckeye, cherry, ash, elm, mulberry, plumb-trees, spicewood, black-haw, red-haw, oak and hickory.

About the time the bucks quit running, Tontileaugo, his wife and children, Tecaughretanego, his son Nungany and myself left the Wiandot camps at the carrying place, and crossed the Sciota river at the south end of the glades, and proceeded on about a south-west course to a large creek called Ollentangy, which I believe interlocks with the waters of the Miami, and empties into Sciota on the west side thereof. From the south end of the prairie to Ollentangy, there is a large quantity of beech land, intermixed with first rate land. Here we made our winter hut, and had considerable success in hunting.

After some time one of Tontileaugo's step-sons, (a lad about eight years of age) offended him, and he gave the boy a moderate whipping, which much displeased his Wiandot wife. She acknowledged that the boy was guilty of a fault, but thought that he ought to have been ducked, which is their usual mode of chastisement. She said she could not bear to have her son whipped like a servant or slave—and she was so displeased that when Tontileaugo went out to hunt, she got her two horses, and all her effects, (as in this country the husband and wife have separate interests) and moved back to the Wiandot camps that we had left.

When Tontileaugo returned, he was much disturbed on hearing of his wife's elopement, and said that he would never go after her were it not that he was afraid that she would get bewildered, and that his children that she had taken with her, might suffer. Tontileaugo went after his wife, and when they met they made up the quarrel, and he never returned; but left Tecaughretanego and his son, (a boy about ten years of age) and myself, who remained here in our hut all winter.

Tecaughretanego who had been a first rate warior, statesman and hunter; and though he was now near sixty years of age, he was yet equal to the common run of hunters, but subject to the rheumatism, which deprived him of the use of his legs.

Shortly after Tontileaugo left us, Tecaughretanego became lame, and could scarcely walk out of our hut for two months. I had considerable success in hunting and trapping. Though Tecaughretanego endured much pain and misery, yet he bore it all with wonderful patience, and would often endeavor to entertain me with chearful conversation. Sometimes he would applaud me for my diligence, skill and activity—and at other times he would take great care in giving me instructions concerning the hunting and trapping business. He would also tell me that if I failed of success, we would suffer very much, as we were about forty miles from any one living, that we knew of; yet he would not intimate that he apprehended we were in any danger, but still supposed that I was fully adequate to the talk.

Tontileaugo left us a little before Christmas, and from that until some time in February, we had always plenty of bear meat, venison, &c. During this time I killed much more than we could use, but having no horses to carry in what I killed, I left part of it in the woods. In February there came a snow, with a crust, which made a great noise when walking on it, and frightened away the deer; and as bear and beaver were scarce here, we got entirely out of provision. After I had hunted two days without eating any thing, and had very short allowance for some days before, I returned late in the evening faint and weary. When I came into our hut, Tecaughretanego asked what success? I told him not any. He asked me if I was not very hungry? I replied that the keen appetite seemed to be in some measure removed, but I was both faint and weary. He commanded Nunganey his little son, to bring me something to eat, and he brought me a kettle with some bones and broth, --after eating a few mouthfuls my appetite violently returned, and I thought the victuals had a most agreeable relish, though it was only fox and wild cat bones, which lay about the camp, which the ravens and turkey-buzzards had picked—these Nunganey had collected and boiled, until the sinews that remained on the bones would strip off. I speedily finished my allowance, such as it was, and when I had ended my *sweet* repast, Tecaughretanego asked me how I felt? I told him that I was much refreshed. He then handed me his pipe and pouch, and told me to take a smoke. I did so. He then said he had something of importance to tell me, if I was now composed and ready to hear it. I told him that I was ready to hear him. He said the reason why he deferred his speech till now was because few men are in a right humor to hear good talk, when they are extremely hungry, as they are then generally fretful and discomposed; but as you appear now to enjoy calmness and serenity of mind, I will now communicate to you the thoughts of my heart, and those things that I know to be true.

"Brother,

"As you have lived with the white people, you have not had the same advantage of knowing that the great being above feeds his people, and gives them their meat in due season, as we Indians have, who are frequently out of provisions, and yet are wonderfully supplied, and that so frequently that it is evidently the hand of the great Owaneeyo* that doth this: whereas the white people have commonly large flocks of tame cattle, that they can kill when they please, and also their barns and cribs filled with grain, and therefore have not the same opportunity of feeling and knowing that they are supported by the ruler of Heaven and Earth.

"Brother,

"I know that you are now afraid that we will all perish with hunger, but you have no just reason to fear this.

"Brother,

"I have been young, but am now old—I have been frequently under the like circumstance that we now are, and that some time or other in almost every year of my life; yet, I have hitherto been supported, and my wants supplied in time of need.

---

* This is the name of God, in their tongue, and signifies the owner and ruler of all things.

"*Brother,*

"Owaneeyo some times suffers us to be in want, in order to teach us our dependence upon him, and to let us know that we are to love and serve him: and like-wise to know the worth of the favors that we receive, and to make us more thankful.

"*Brother,*

"Be assured that you will be supplied with food, and that just in the right time; but you must continue diligent in the use of means—go to sleep, and rise early in the morning and go a hunting—be strong and exert yourself like a man, and the great spirit will direct your way."

The next morning I went out, and steered about an east course. I proceeded on slowly for about five miles, and saw deer frequently, but as the crust on the snow made a great noise, they were always running before I spied them, so that I could not get a shoot. A violent appetite returned, and I became intolerably hungry; --it was now that I concluded I would run off to Pennsylvania, my native country. As the snow was on the ground, and Indian hunters almost the whole of the way before me, I had but a poor prospect of making my escape; but my case appeared desperate. If I staid here I thought I would perish with hunger, and if I met with Indians, they could but kill me.

I then proceeded on as fast as I could walk, and when I got about ten or twelve miles from our hut, I came upon fresh buffaloe tracks, -- I pursued after, and in a short time came in sight of them, as they were passing through a small glade—I ran with all my might, and headed them, where I lay in ambush, and killed a very large cow. I immediately kindled a fire and began to roast meat, but could not wait till it was done—I ate it almost raw. When hunger was abated I began to be tenderly concerned for my old Indian brother, and the little boy I had left in a perishing condition. I made haste and packed up what meat I could carry, secured what I left from the wolves, and returned homewards.

I scarcely thought on the old man's speech while I was almost distracted with hunger, but on my return was much affected with it, reflected on myself for my hard-heartedness and ingratitude, in attempting to run off and leave the venerable old man and little boy to perish with hunger. I also considered how remarkably the old man's speech had been verified in our providentially obtaining a supply. I thought also of that part of his speech which treated of the fractious dispositions of hungry people, which was the only excuse I had for my base inhumanity, in attempting to leave them in the most deplorable situation.

As it was moon-light, I got home to our hut, and found the old man in his usual good humor. He thanked me for my exertion, and bid me sit down, as I must certainly be fatigued, and he commanded Nunganey to make haste and cook. I told him I would cook for him, and let the boy lay some meat on the coals, for himself—which he did, but ate it almost raw, as I had done. I immediately hung on the kettle with some water, and cut the beef in thin slices, and put them in: -- when it had boiled awhile, I proposed taking it off the fire, but the old man replied, "let it be done enough." This he said in as patient and unconcerned a manner, as if he had not wanted one single meal. He commanded Nunganey to eat no more beef at that time, least he might hurt himself; but told him to sit down, and after some time he might sup some broth—this command he reluctantly obeyed.

When we were all refreshed, Tecaughretanego delivered a speech upon the necessity and pleasure of receiving the necessary supports of life with thankfulness, knowing that Owaneeyo is the great giver. Such speeches from an Indian, may be tho't by those who are unacquainted with them, altogether incredible; but when we reflect on the Indian war, we may readily conclude that they are not an ignorant or stupid sort of people, or they would not have been such fatal enemies. When they came into our country they outwitted us—and when we sent armies into their country, they outgeneralled, and beat us with inferior force. Let us also take into consideration that Tecaughretanego was no common person, but was among the Indians, as Socrates in the ancient Heathen world; and it may be, equal to him—if not in wisdom and learning, yet, perhaps in patience and fortitude. Notwithstanding Tecaughretanego's uncommon natural abilities, yet in the sequel of this history you will see the deficiency of the light of nature, unaided by revelation, in this truly great man.

The next morning Tecaughretanego desired me to go back and bring another load of buffaloe beef: As I proceeded to do so, about five miles from our hut I found a bear tree. As a sapling grew near the tree, and reached near the hole that the bear went in at, I got dry dozed or rotten wood, that would catch and hold fire almost as well as spunk. This wood I tied up in bunches, fixed them on my back, and then climbed up the sapling, and with a pole, I put them touched with fire, into the hole, and then came down and took my gun in my hand. After some time the bear came out, and I killed and skinned it, packed up a load of the meat, (after securing the remainder from the wolves) and returned home before night. On my return my old brother and his son were much rejoiced at my success. After this we had plenty of provision.

We remained here until some time in April 1758. At this time Tecaughretanego had recovered so, that he could walk about. We made a bark canoe, embarked, and went down Ollentangy some distance, but the water being low, we were in danger of splitting our canoe upon the rocks: therefore Tecaughretanego concluded we would encamp on shore, and pray for rain.

When we encamped, Tecaughretanego made himself a sweat-house; which he did by sticking a number of hoops in the ground, each hoop forming a semi-circle—this he covered all round with blankets and skins; he then prepared hot stones, which he rolled into this hut, and then went into it himself, with a little kettle of water in his hand, mixed with a variety of herbs, which he had formerly cured, and had now with him in his pack—they afforded an odoriferous perfume. When he was in, he told me to pull down the blankets behind him, and cover all up close, which I did, and then he began to pour water upon the hot stones, and to sing aloud. He continued in this vehement hot place about fifteen minutes: –all this he did in order to purify himself before he would address the Supreme Being. When he came out of his sweat-house, he began to burn tobacco and to pray. He began each petition with *oh, ho, ho, ho,* which is a kind of aspiration, and signifies an ardent wish. I observed that all his petitions were only for immediate, or present temporal blessings. He began his address by thanksgiving, in the following manner:

"O great being! I thank thee that I have obtained the use of my legs again—that I am now able to walk about and kill turkeys, &c. without feeling exquisite pain and misery: I know that thou art a hearer and a helper, and therefore I will call upon thee.

"Oh, ho, ho, ho,

"Grant that my knees and ancles may be right well, and that I may be able, not only to walk, but to run, and to jump logs, as I did last fall.

"Oh, ho, ho, ho,

"Grant that on this voyage we may frequently kill bears, as they may be crossing the Sciota and Sandusky.

"Oh, ho, ho, ho,

"Grant that we may kill plenty of Turkeys along the banks, to stew with our fat bear meat.

"Oh, ho, ho, ho,

"Grant that rain may come to raise the Ollentangy about two or three feet, that we may cross in safety down to Sciota, without danger of our canoe being wrecked on the rocks; —and now, O great being! thou knowest that I am a great lover of tobacco, and though I know not when I may get any more, I now make a present of the last I have unto thee, as a free burnt offering; therefore I expect thou wilt hear and grant these requests, and I thy servant will return thee thanks, and love thee for thy gifts."

During the whole of this scene I sat by Tecaughretanego, and as he went through it with the greatest solemnity, I was seriously affected with his prayers. I remained duly composed until he came to the burning of the tobacco, and as I knew that he was a great lover of it, and saw him cast the last of it into the fire, it excited in me a kind of meriment, and I insensibly smiled. Tecaughretanego observed me laughing, which displeased him, and occasioned him to address me in the following manner.

"Brother,

"I have somewhat to say to you, and I hope you will not be offended when I tell you of your faults. You know that when you were reading your books in town, I would not let the boys or any one disturb you; but now when I was praying, I saw you laughing. I do not think that you look upon praying as a foolish thing; —I believe you pray yourself. But perhaps you may think my mode, or manner of prayer foolish; if so, you ought in a friendly manner to instruct me, and not make sport of sacred things.

I acknowledged my error, and on this he handed me his pipe to smoke, in token of friendship and reconciliation; though at that time he had nothing to smoke, but red-willow bark. I told him something of the method of reconciliation with an offended God, as revealed in my Bible, which I had then in possession. He said that he liked my story better than that of the French priests, but he thought that he was now too old to begin to learn a new religion, therefore he should continue to worship God in the way that he had been taught, and that if salvation or future happiness was to be had in his way of worship, he expected he would obtain it, and if it was inconsistent with the honor of the great spirit to accept of him in his own way of worship, he hoped that Owaneeyo would accept of him in the way I had mentioned, or in some other way, though he might now be ignorant of the channel through which favor or mercy might be conveyed. He said that he believed that Owaneeyo would hear and help every one that sincerely waited upon him.

Here we may see how far the light of nature could go; perhaps we see it here almost in its highest extent. Notwithstanding the just views that this great man entertained of Providence, yet we now see him (although he acknowledged his guilt) expecting to appease the Deity, and procure his favor, by burning a little tobacco. We may observe that all Heathen nations, as far as we can find out either by tradition or the light of Nature, agree with Revelation in this, that sacrifice is necessary, or that some kind of atonement is to be made, in order to remove guilt, and reconcile them to God. This, accompanied with numberless other witnesses, is sufficient evidence of the rationality the truth of the Scriptures.

A few days after Tecaughretanego had gone through his ceremonies, and finished his prayers, the rain came and raised the creek a sufficient height, so that we passed in safety down to Sciota, and proceeded up to the carrying place. Let us now describe the land on this route, from our winter hut, and down Ollentangy to the Sciota, and up it to the carrying place.

About our winter cabbin is chiefly first and second rate land. A considerable way up Ollentangy on the south-west side thereof, or betwixt it and the Miami, there is a very large prairie, and from this prairie down Ollentangy to Sciota, is generally first rate land. The timber is walnut, sugar-tree, ash, buckeye, locust, wild-cherry, and spice-wood, intermixed with some oak and beech. From the mouth of Ollentangy on the east side of Sciota, up to the carrying place, there is a large body of first and second rate land, and tolerably well watered. The timber is ash, sugar-tree, walnut, locust, oak, and beech. Up near the carrying place, the land is a little hilly, but the soil is good.

We proceeded from this place down Sandusky, and in our passage we killed four bears, and a number of turkeys. Tecaughretanego appeared now fully persuaded that all this came in answer to his prayers—and who can say with any degree of certainty that it was not so?

When we came to the little lake at the mouth of Sandusky we called at a Wiandot town that was then there, called Sunyendeand. Here we diverted ourselves several days, by catching rock-fish in a small creek, the name of which is also Sunyendeand, which signifies Rock-Fish.

They fished in the night, with lights, and struck the fish with giggs or spears. The rock-fish here, when they begin first to run up the creek to spawn, are exceeding fat, and sufficient to fry themselves. The first night we scarcely caught fish enough for present use, for all that was in the town.

The next morning I met with a prisoner at this place, by the name of Thompson, who had been taken from Virginia: he told me if the Indians would only omit disturbing the fish for one night, he could catch more fish than the whole town could make use of. I told Mr. Thompson that if he was certain that he could do this, that I would use my influence with the Indians, to let the fish alone for one night. I applied to the chiefs, who agreed to my proposal, and said they were anxious to see what the Great Knife (as they called the Virginian) could do. Mr. Thompson, with the assistance of some other prisoners, set to work, and made a hoop net of Elm bark: they then cut down a tree across the creek, and stuck in stakes at the lower side of it, to prevent the fish from passing up, leaving only a gap at the one side of the creek: —here he sat with his net, and when he felt the fish touch the net he drew it up, and frequently would hawl out two or three rock-fish that would weigh about five or six pounds each. He continued at this until he had hawled out about a waggon load, and then left the gap open, in order to let them pass up, for they could not go far, on account of the shallow water. Before day Mr. Thompson shut it up, to prevent them from passing down, in order to let the Indians have some diversion in killing them in daylight.

When the news of the fish came to town, the Indians all collected, and with surprize beheld the large heap of fish, and applauded the ingenuity of the Virginian. When they saw the number of them that were confined in the water above the tree, the young Indians ran back to the town, and in a short time returned with their spears, giggs, bows and arrows, &c. and were the chief of that day engaged in killing rock-fish, insomuch that we had more than we could use or preserve. As we had no salt, or any way to keep them, they lay upon the banks, and after some time great numbers of turkey-buzzards and eagles collected together and devoured them.

Shortly after this we left Sunyendeand, and in three days arrived at Detroit, where we remained this summer.

Some time in May we heard that General Forbes, with seven thousand men was preparing to carry on a campaign against Fort DuQuesne, which then stood near where Fort Pitt was afterwards erected. Upon receiving this news a number of runners were sent off by the French commander at Detroit, to urge the different tribes of Indian warriors to repair to Fort DuQuesne.

Some time in July 1758, the Ottowas, Jibewas, Potowatomies and Wiandots rendezvoused at Detroit, and marched off to Fort DuQuesne, to prepare for the encounter of General Forbes. The common report was, that they would serve him as they did General Braddock, and obtain much plunder. From this time, until fall, we had frequent accounts of Forbes's army, by Indian runners that were sent out to watch their motion. They spied them frequently from the mountains ever after they left Fort Loudon. Notwithstanding their vigilance, colonel Grant with his Highlanders stole a march upon them, and in the night took possession of a hill about eight rod from Fort DuQuesne: –this hill is on that account called Grant's hill to this day. The French and Indians knew not that Grant and his men were there until they beat the drum and played upon the bag-pipes, just at day-light. They then flew to arms, and the Indians ran up under covert of the banks of Allegheny and Monongahela, for some distance, and then sallied out from the banks of the rivers, and took possession of the hill above Grant; and as he was on the point of it in sight of the fort, they immediately surrounded him, and as he had his Highlanders in ranks, and very close order, and the Indians scattered, and concealed behind trees, they defeated him with the loss only of a few warriors: –most of the Highlanders were killed or taken prisoners.

After this defeat the Indians held a council, but were divided in their opinions. Some said that general Forbes would now turn back, and go home the way that he came, as Dunbar had done with General Braddock was defeated: others supposed he would come on. The French urged the Indians to stay and see the event: –but as it was hard for the Indians to be absent from their squaws and children, at the season of the year, a great many of them returned home to their hunting. After this, the remainder of the Indians, some French regulars, and a number of Canadians, marched off in quest of General Forbes. They met his army near Fort Ligoneer, and attacked them, but were frustrated in their design. They said that Forbes's men were beginning to learn the art of war, and that there were a great number of American riflemen along with the red-coats, who scattered out, took trees, and were good marks-men; therefore they found they could not accomplish their design, and were obliged to retreat. When they returned from the battle to Fort DuQuesne, the Indians concluded that they would go to the hunting. The French endeavored to persuade them to stay and try another battle. The Indians said if it was only the red-coats they had to do with, they could soon subdue them, but they could not withstand *Ashalecoa*, or the Great Knife, which was the name they gave the Virginians. They then returned home to their hunting, and the French evacuated the fort, which General Forbes came and took possession of without further opposition, late in the year 1758, and at this time began to build Fort Pitt.

When Tecaughretanego had heard the particulars of Grant's defeat, he said that he could not well account for his contradictory and inconsistent conduct. He said as the art of war consists in ambushing and surprizing our enemies, and in preventing them from ambushing and surprizing us; Grant, in the first place, acted like a wife and experienced officer, in artfully approaching in the night without being discovered; but when he came to the place, and the Indians were lying asleep outside of the fort, between him and the Allegheny river, in place of slipping up quietly, and falling upon them with their broad swords, they beat the drums and played upon the bag-pipes. He said he could account for this inconsistent conduct no other way than by supposing that he had made too free with spirituous liquors during the night, and became intoxicated about day-light. But to return:

This year we hunted up Sandusky, and down Sciota, took nearly the same route that we had done the last hunting season. We had considerable success, and returned to Detroit some time in April 1759.

Shortly after this, Tecaughretanego, his son Nungany and myself, went from Detroit, (in an elm bark canoe) to Caughnewaga, a very ancient Indian town, about nine miles above Montreal, where I remained until about the first of July. I then heard of a French ship at Montreal that had English prisoners on board, in order to carry them over sea, and exchange them. I went privately off from the Indians, and got also on board; but as general Wolfe had stopped the River St. Laurence, we were all sent to prison at Montreal, where I remained four months. Some time in November we were all sent off from this place to Crown Point, and exchanged.

Early in the year 1760, I came home to Conococheague, and found that my people could never ascertain whether I was killed or taken, until my return. They received me with great joy, but were surprised to see me so much like an Indian, both in my gait and gesture.

Upon enquiry, I found that my sweet-heart was married a few days before I arrived. My feelings I must leave on this occasion, for those of my readers to judge, who have felt the pangs of disappointed love, as it is impossible now for me to describe the emotion of soul I felt at that time.

Now there was peace with the Indians which lasted until the year 1763. Sometime in May, this year, I married, and about that time the Indians again commenced hostilities, and were busily engaged in killing and scalping the frontier inhabitants in various parts of Pennsylvania. The whole Conococheague Valley, from the North to the South Mountain, had been almost entirely evacuated during Braddock's war. This state was then a Quaker government, and at the first of this war the frontiers received no assistance from the state. As the people were now beginning to live at home again, they thought hard to be drove away a second time, and were determined if possible, to make a stand: therefore they raised as much money by collections and subscriptions, as would pay a company of rifle-men for several months. The subscribers met and elected a committee to manage the business. The committee appointed me captain of this company of rangers, and gave me the appointment of my subalterns. I chose two of the most active young men that I could find, who had also been long in captivity with the Indians. As we enlisted our men, we dressed them uniformly in the Indian manner, with breech-clouts, leggins, mockasons and green shrouds, which we wore in the same manner that the Indians do, and nearly as the Highlanders wear their plaids. In place of hats we wore red handkerchiefs, and painted our faces red and black, like Indian warriors. I taught them the Indian discipline, as I knew of no other at that time, which would answer the purpose much better than British. We succeeded beyond expectation in defending the frontiers, and were extolled by our employers. Near the conclusion of this expedition, I accepted of an ensign's commission in the regular service, under King George, in what was then called the Pennsylvania line. Upon my resignation, my lieutenant succeeded me in command, the rest of the time they were to serve. In the fall (the same year) I went on the Susquehannah campaign, against the Indians, under the command of General Armstrong. In this route we burnt the Delaware and Monsey towns, on the West Branch of the Susquehannah, and destroyed all their corn.

In the year 1764, I received a lieutenant's commission, and went out on General Bouquet's campaign against the Indians on the Muskingum. Here we brought them to terms, and promised to be at peace with them, upon condition that they would give up all our people that they had then in captivity among them. They then delivered unto us three hundred of the prisoners, and said that they could not collect them all at this time, as it was now late in the year, and they were far scattered; but they promised that they would bring them all into Fort Pitt early next spring, and a security that they would do this, they delivered to us six of their chiefs, as hostages. Upon this we settled a cessation of arms for six months, and promised upon their fulfilling the aforesaid condition, to make with them a permanent peace.

A little below Fort Pitt the hostages all made their escape. Shortly after this the Indians stole horses, and killed some people on the frontiers. The king's proclamation was then circulating and set up in various public places, prohibiting any person from trading with the Indians, until further orders.

Notwithstanding all this, about the first of March 1765, a number of waggons loaded with Indian goods, and warlike stores, were sent from Philadelphia to Henry Pollen's, Conococheague, and from thence seventy pack-horses were loaded with these goods, in order to carry them to Fort Pitt. This alarmed the country, and Mr. William Duffield raised about fifty armed men, and met the pack-horses at the place where Mercersburg now stands. Mr. Duffield desired the employers to store up their goods, and not proceed until further orders. They made light of this, and went over the North Mountain, where they lodged in a small valley called the Great Cove. Mr. Duffield and his party followed after, and came to their lodging, and again urged them to store up their goods: –He reasoned with them on the impropriety of their proceedings, and the great danger the frontier inhabitants would be exposed to, if the Indians should now get a supply: –He said as it was well known that they had scarcely any amunition, and were almost naked, to supply them now, would be a kind of murder, and would be illegally trading at the expence of the blood and treasure of the frontiers. Notwithstanding his powerful reasoning, these traders made game of what he said, and would only answer him by ludicrous burlesque.

When I beheld this, and found that Mr. Duffield would not compel them to store up their goods, I collected ten of my old warriors, that I had formerly disciplined in the Indian way, went off privately, after night, and encamped in the woods. The next day, as usual, we blacked and painted, and waylayed them near Sidelong Hill. I scattered my men about forty rod along the side of the road, and ordered every two to take a tree, and about eight or ten rod between each couple, with orders to keep a reserve fire, one not to fire until his comrade had loaded his gun—by this means we kept up a constant, slow fire, upon them from front to rear: –We then heard nothing of these trader's merriment or burlesque. When they saw their pack-horses falling close by them, they called out *pray gentlemen, what would you have us to do?* The reply was, *collect all your loads to the front, and unload them in one place; take your private property, and immediately retire.* When they were gone, we burnt what they left, which consisted of blankets, shirts, vermillion, lead, beads, wampum, tomahawks, scalping knives, &c.

The traders went back to Fort Loudon, and applied to the commanding officer there, and got a party of Highland soldiers, and went with them in quest of the robbers, as they called us, and without applying to a magistrate, or obtaining any civil authority, but barely upon suspicion, they took a number of creditable persons prisoners, (who were chiefly not in any way concerned in this action) and confined them in the guard-house in Fort Loudon. I then raised three hundred riflemen, marched to Fort Loudon, and encamped on a hill in sight of the fort. We were not long there, until we had more than double as many of the British troops prisoners in our camp, as they had of our people in the guard-house. Captain Grant, a Highland officer, who commanded Fort Loudon, then sent a flag of truce to our camp, where we settled a cartel, and gave them above two for one, which enabled us to redeem all our men from the guard-house, without further difficulty.

After this Captain Grant kept a number of rifle guns, which the Highlanders had taken from the country people, and refused to give them up. As he was riding out one day, we took him prisoner, and detained him until he delivered up the arms; we also destroyed a large quantity of gun-powder that the traders had stored up, lest it might be conveyed privately to the Indians. The king's troops, and our party, had now got entirely out of the channel of the civil law, and many unjustifiable things were done by both parties. This convinced me more than ever I had been before, of the absolute necessity of the civil law, in order to govern mankind.

About this time the following song was composed by Mr. George Campbell (an Irish gentleman, who had been educated in Dublin) and was frequently sung to the tune of the Black Joke:

1. Ye patriot souls who love to sing,
   What serves your country and your king,
       In wealth, peace and royal estate;
   Attention give whilst I rehearse,
   A modern fact, in jingling verse,
   How party interest strove what it cou'd,
   To profit itself by public blood,
       But justly met its merited fate.

2. Let all those Indian traders claim,
   Their just reward, inglorious fame,
       For vile base and treacherous ends.
   To Pollins, in the spring they sent,
   Much warlike stores, with an intent,
   To carry them to our barbarous foes,
   Expecting that no-body dare oppose,
       A present to their Indian friends.

3. Astonish'd at the wild design,
   Frontier inhabitants combin'd,
       With brave souls, to stop their career,
   Although some men apostatiz'd,
   Who first the grand attempt advis'd,
   The bold frontiers they bravely stood,
   To act for their king and their country's good,
       in joint league, and strangers to fear.

4. On March the fifth, in sixty-five,
   Their Indian presents did arrive,
       in long pomp and cavalcade,
   Near Sidelong Hill, where in disguise,
   Some patriots did their train surprize,
   And quick as lightning tumbled their loads,
   And kindled them bonfires in the woods,
       And mostly burnt their whole brigade.

> 5. *At Loudon, when they heard the news,*
>   *They scarcely knew which way to choose,*
>   *For blind rage and discontent;*
>   *At length some soldiers they sent out,*
>   *With guides for to conduct the route,*
>   *And seized some men that were trav'ling there,*
>   *And hurried them into Loudon where*
>   *They laid them fast with one consent.*
>
> 6. *But men of resolution thought,*
>   *Too much to see their neighbors caught,*
>   *For no crime but false surmise;*
>   *Forthwith they join'd a warlike band,*
>   *And march'd to Loudon out of hand,*
>   *And kept the jailors pris'ners there,*
>   *Until our friends enlarged were,*
>   *Without fraud or any disguise.*
>
> 7. *Let mankind censure or commend,*
>   *This rash performance in the end,*
>   *Then both sides will find their account.*
>   *'Tis true no law can justify,*
>   *To burn our neighbors property,*
>   *But when this property is design'd,*
>   *To serve the enemies of mankind,*
>   *It's high treason in the amount.*

After this we kept up a guard of men on the frontiers, for several months, to prevent supplies being sent to the Indians, until it was proclaimed that Sir William Johnson had made peace with them, and then we let the traders pass unmolested.

In the year 1766, I heard that Sir William Johnson, the king's agent for settling affairs with the Indians, had purchased from them all the land west of the Appalachian Mountains, that lay between the Ohio and the Cherokee River; and as I knew by conversing with the Indians in their own tongue, that there was a large body of rich land there, I concluded I would take a tour westward, and explore that country.

I set out about the last of June, 1766, and went in the first place to Holstein River, and from thence I travelled westward in company with Joshua Horton, Uriah Stone, William Baker, and James Smith, who came from near Carlisle. There was only four white men of us, and a mulatto slave about eighteen years of age, that Mr. Horton had with him. We explored the country south of Kentucky, and there was no more sign of white men there then, than there is now west of the head waters of the Missouri. We also explored Cumberland and Tennessee Rivers, from Stone's* River down to the Ohio.

When we came to the mouth of Tennessee my fellow travellers concluded that they would proceed on to the Illinois, and see some more of the land to the west: –this I would not agree to. As I had already been longer from home than what I expected, I thought my wife would be distressed, and think I was killed by the Indians; therefore I concluded that I would return home. I sent my horse with my fellow travellers to the Illinois, as it was difficult to take a horse through the mountains. My comrades gave me the greatest part of the amunition they then had, which amounted only to half a pound of powder, and lead equivalent. Mr. Horton also lent me his mulatto boy, and I then set off through the wilderness, for Carolina.

About eight days after I left my company at the mouth of the Tennessee, on my journey eastward, I got a cane stab in my foot, which occasioned my leg to swell, and I suffered much pain. I was now in a doleful situation—far from any of the human species, excepting black Jamie, or the savages, and I knew not when I might meet with them—my case appeared desperate, and I thought some thing must be done. All the surgical instruments I had, was a knife, a mockason awl, and a pair of bullit moulds—with these I determined to draw the snag from my foot, if possible. I stuck the awl in the skin, and with the knife I cut the flesh away from around the cane, and then I commanded the mulatto fellow to catch it with the bullit moulds, and pull it out, which he did. When I saw it, it seemed a shocking thing to be in any person's foot; it will therefore be supposed that I was very glad to have it out. The black fellow attended upon me, and obeyed my directions faithfully. I ordered him to search for Indian medicine, and told him to get me a quantity of bark from the root of a lynn tree, which I made him beat on a stone, with a tomahawk, and boil it in a kettle, and with the ooze I bathed my foot and leg: –what remained when I had finished bathing, I boiled to a jelly, and made poultices

---

* Stone's River is a south branch of Cumberland, and empties into it above Nashville. We first gave it this name in our journal in May 1767, after one of my fellow travelers, Mr. Uriah Stone, and I am told that it retains the same name unto this day.

thereof. As I had no rags, I made use of the green moss that grows upon logs, and wrapped it round with elm bark: by this means (simple as it may seem) the swelling and inflammation in a great measure abated. As stormy weather appeared, I order Jamie to make us a shelter, which he did by erecting forks and poles, and covering them over with cane tops, like a sodder-house. It was but about one hundred yards from a large buffaloe road. As we were almost out of provision, I commanded Jamie to take my gun, and I went along as well as I could, concealed myself near the road, and killed a buffaloe. When this was done, we jirked* the lean, and fryed the tallow out of the fat meat, which we kept to stew with our jirk as we needed it.

While I lay at this place, all the books I had to read, was a Psalm Book, and Watts upon Prayer. Whilst in this situation I composed the following verses, which I then frequently sung.

1. *Six weeks I've in this desart been,*
    With one mulatto lad,
  Excepting this poor stupid slave,
    No company I had.

2. *In solitude I here remain,*
    A cripple very sore,
  No friend or neighbor to be found,
    My case for to deplore.

3. *I'm far from home, far from the wife,*
    Which in my bosom lay,
  Far from my children dear, which used
    Around me for to play.

4. *This doleful circumstance cannot*
    My happiness prevent,
  While peace of conscience I enjoy,
    Great comfort and content.

---

* Jirk is a name well known by the hunters, and frontier inhabitants, for meat cut in small pieces and laid on a scaffold, over a slow fire, whereby it is roasted till it is thoroughly dry.

I continued in this place until I could walk slowly, without crutches. As I now lay near a great buffaloe road, I was afraid that the Indians might be passing that way, and discover my fire-place, therefore I moved off some distance, where I remained until I killed an elk. As my foot was yet sore, I concluded that I would stay here until it was healed, lest by travelling too soon it might again be inflamed.

In a few weeks after, I proceeded on, and in October I arrived in Carolina. I had now been eleven months in the wilderness, and during this time I neither saw bread, money, women, or spirituous liquors; and three months of which I saw none of the human species, except Jamie.

When I came into the settlement my clothes were almost worn out, and the boy had nothing on him that ever was spun. He had buck-skin leggins, mockasons, and breech-clout—a bear-skin dressed with the hair on, which he belted about him, and a racoon-skin cap. I had not travelled far after I came in before I was strictly examined by the inhabitants. I told them the truth, and where I came from, &c. but my story appeared to be strange to them, that they did not believe me. They said they had never heard of any one coming through the mountains from the mouth of Tennessee; and if any one would undertake such a journey, surely no man would lend him his slave. They said that they thought all I had told them were lies, and on suspicion they took me into custody, and set a guard over me.

While I was confined here, I met with a reputable old acquaintance, who voluntarily became my voucher; and also told me of a number of my acquaintances that now lived near this place, who had moved from Pennsylvania—On this being made public, I was liberated. I went to a magistrate, and obtained a pass, and one of my old acquaintances made me a present of a shirt. I then cast away my old rags, and all the clothes I now had was an old beaver hat, buck-skin leggins, mockasons, and a new shirt; also an old blanket, which I commonly carried on my back in good weather. Being thus equipped, I marched on, with my white shirt loose, and Jamie with his bear-skin about him:—myself appearing white, and Jamie very black, alarmed the dogs where-ever we came, so that they barked violently. The people frequently came out and asked me where we came from, &c. I told them the truth, but they, for the most part suspected my story, and I generally had to shew them my pass. In this way I came on to Fort Chissel, where I left Jamie at Mr. Horton's negro-quarter, according to promise.

I went from thence to Mr. George Adams's, on Reed Creek, where I had lodged, and where I had left my clothes, as I was going out from home. When I dressed myself in good clothes, and mounted on horseback, no man ever asked me for a pass; therefore I concluded that a horse-thief, or even a robber, might pass without interruption, provided he was only well-dressed, whereas the shabby villain would be immediately detected.

I returned home to Conococheague, in the fall 1767. When I arrived, I found that my wife and friends had despaired of ever seeing me again, as they had heard that I was killed by the Indians, and my horse brought into one of the Cherokee towns.

In the year 1769, the Indians again made incursions on the frontiers; yet, the traders continued carrying goods and warlike stores to them. The frontiers took the alarm, and a number of persons collected, destroyed and plundered a quantity of their powder, lead, &c. in Bedford county. Shortly after this, some of these persons, with others, were apprehended and laid in irons in the guard-house in Fort Bedford, on suspicion of being the perpetrators of this crime.

Though I did not altogether approve of the conduct of this new club of black-boys, yet I concluded that they should not lie in irons in the guard-house, or remain in confinement, by arbitrary or military power. I resolved therefore, if possible, to release them, if they even should be tried by the civil law afterwards. I collected eighteen of my old black-boys, that I had seen tried in the Indian war, &c. I did not desire a large party, lest they should be too much alarmed at Bedford, and accordingly prepare for us. We marched along the public road in day-light, and made no secret of our design: —We told those whom we met, that we were going to take Fort Bedford, which appeared to them a very unlikely story. Before this I made it known to one William Thompson, a man whom I could trust, and who lived there: him I employed as a spy, and sent him along on horse-back, before, with orders to meet me at a certain place near Bedford, one hour before day. The next day a little before sun-set we encamped near the crossings of Juniata, about fourteen miles from Bedford, and erected tents, as though we intended staying all night, and not a man in my company knew to the contrary, save myself. Knowing that they would hear this in Bedford, and wishing it to be the case, I thought to surprize them, by stealing a march.

As the moon rose about eleven o'clock, I ordered my boys to march, and we went on at the rate of five miles an hour, until we met Thompson at the place appointed. He told us that the commanding officer had frequently heard of us by travelers, and had ordered thirty men upon guard. He said they knew our number, and only made game of the notion of eighteen men coming to rescue the prisoners, but they did not expect us until towards the middle of the day. I asked him if the gate was open? He said it was then shut, but he expected they would open it as usual, at day-light, as they apprehended no danger. I then moved my men privately up under the banks of Juniata, where we lay concealed about one hundred yards from the fort gate. I had ordered the men to keep a profound silence, until we got into it. I then sent off Thompson again to spy. At day-light he returned, and told us that the gate was open, and three centinels were standing on the wall—that the guards were taking a morning dram, and the arms standing together in one place. I then concluded to rush into the fort, and told Thompson to run before me to the arms, we ran with all our might, and as it was a misty morning, the centinels scarcely saw us until we were within the gate, and took possession of the arms. Just as we were entering, two of them discharged their guns, though I do not believe they aimed at us. We then raised a shout, which surprized the town, though some of them were well pleased with the news. We compelled a black-smith to take the irons off the prisoners, and then we left the place. This, I believe, was the first British fort in America, that was taken by what they called American rebels.

Some time after this I took a journey westward, in order to survey some located land I had on and near the Youhogany. As I passed near Bedford, while I was walking and leading my horse, I was overtaken by some men on horse-back, like travellers. One of them asked my name, and on telling it, they immediately pulled out their pistols, and presented them at me, calling upon me to deliver myself, or I was a dead man. I stepped back, presented my rifle, and told them to stand off. One of them snapped a pistol at me, and another was preparing to shoot, when I fired my piece: —one of them also fired near the same time, and one of my fellow travellers fell. The assailants then rushed up, and as my gun was empty, they took and tied me. I charged them with killing my fellow traveller, and told them he was a man that I had accidentally met with on the road, that had nothing to do with the public quarrel. They asserted that I had killed him. I told them that my gun blowed, or made a slow fire—that I had her from my face before she went off, or I would not have missed my mark; and from the position my piece was in when it went off, it was not likely that my gun killed this man, yet I acknowledged I was not certain that it was not so. They then carried me to Bedford, laid me in irons in the guard-house, summoned a jury of the opposite party, and held an inquest. The jury brought me in guilty of wilful murder. As they were afraid to keep me long in Bedford, for fear of a rescue, they sent me privately through the wilderness to Carlisle, where I was laid in heavy irons.

Shortly after I came here, we heard that a number of my old black-boys were coming to tear down the jail. I told the sheriff that I would not be rescued, as I knew that the indictment was wrong; therefore I wished to stand my trial. As I had found the black boys to be always under good command, I expected I could prevail on them to return, and therefore wished to write to them—to this the sheriff readily agreed. I wrote a letter to them, with irons on my hands, which was immediately sent; but as they had heard that I was in irons, they would come on. When we heard they were near the town, I told the sheriff I would speak to them out of the window, and if the irons were off, I made no doubt but I could prevail on them to desist. The sheriff ordered them to be taken off, and just as they were taken off my hands, the black boys came running up to the jail. I went to the window and called to them, and they gave attention. I told them as my indictment was for wilful murder, to admit of being rescued, would appear dishonorable. I thanked them for their kind intentions, and told them the greatest favor they could confer upon me, would be to grant me this one request, *to withdraw from the jail, and return in peace*; to this they complied, and withdrew. While I was speaking, the irons were taken off my feet, and never again put on.

Before this party arrived at Conococheague, they met about three hundred more, on the way, coming to their assistance, and were resolved to take me out; they then turned, and all came together, to Carlisle. The reason they gave for coming again, was, because they thought that government was so enraged at me that I would not get a fair trial; but my friends and myself together again prevailed on them to return in peace.

At this time the public papers were partly filled with these occurrences. The following is an extract from the Pennsylvania Gazette, number 2132, November 2d, 1769.

"*Conococheague, October 16th, 1769.*

" Mess. Hall & Sellers

" Please to give the following narrative a place in your Gazette, and you will much oblige

" Your humble servant,
" WILLIAM SMITH. "

" Whereas, in this Gazette of September 28th, 1769, there appeared an extract of a letter from Bedford, September 12th, 1769, relative to James Smith, as being apprehended on suspicion of being a black boy, then killing his companion, &c. I look upon myself as bound by all the obligations of truth, justice to character and to the world, to set that matter in a true light; by which, I hope the impartial world will be enabled to obtain a more just opinion of the present scheme of acting in this end of the country, as also to form a true idea of the truth, candor, and ingenuity of the author of the said extract, in stating that matter in so partial a light. The state of the case (which can be made appear by undeniable evidence,) was this: "James Smith, (who is stiled the principal ring leader of the black boys, by the said author) together with his younger brother, and brother-in-law, were going out in order to survey and improve their land on the waters of Youghoghany, and as the time of their return was long, they took with them their arms, and horses loaded with the necessaries of life: and as one of Smith's brothers-in-law was an artist in surveying, he had also with him the instruments for that business. Travelling on the way, within about nine miles of Bedford, they overtook, and joined company with one Johnson and Moorhead, who likewise had horses loaded, part of which loading was liquor, and part seed wheat, their intention being to make improvements on their lands. When they arrived at the parting of the road on this side of Bedford, the company separated, one part going through the town, in order to get a horse shod, were apprehended, and put under confinement, but for what crime they knew not, and treated in a manner utterly inconsistent with the laws of their country, and the liberties of Englishmen: –Whilst the other part, viz. James Smith, Johnson and Moorhead, taking along the other road, were met by John Holmes esq. to whom James Smith spoke in a friendly manner, but received no answer. Mr. Holmes hasted, and gave an alarm in Bedford, from whence a party of men were sent in pursuit of them; but Smith and his companions not having the least thought of any such measures being taken, (why should they?) travelled slowly on. After they had gained the place where the roads joined, they delayed until the other part of their company should come up. At this time a number of men came riding, like men travelling; they asked Smith his name, which he told them—on which they immediately assaulted him as highway-men, and with presented pistols, commanded him to surrender, or he was a dead man; upon which Smith stepped back, asked them if they were highway-men, charging them at the same time to stand off, when immediately, Robert George (one of the assailants) snapped a pistol at Smith's head, and that before Smith offered to shoot, (which said George himself acknowledged upon oath;) whereupon Smith presented his gun at another of the assailants, who was preparing to shoot him with his pistol. The said assailant having a hold of Johnson by the arm, two shots were fired, one by Smith's gun, the other from a pistol so quick as just to be distinguishable, and Johnson fell. After which Smith was taken and carried into Bedford, where John Holmes, esq. the informer, held an inquest on the corpse, one of the assailants being as an evidence, (nor was there any other trouble about the matter) Smith was brought in guilty of wilful murder, and so committed to prison. But a jealousy arising in the breasts of many that the inquest, either through inadvertency, ignorance or some other default, was not so fair as it ought to be; William Deny, coroner of the county, upon requisition made, thought proper to re-examine the matter, and summoning a jury of unexceptionable men, out of three townships—men whose candor, probity and honesty, is unquestionable with all who are acquainted with them, and having raised the corpse, held an inquest in a solemn manner, during three days. In the course of their scrutiny they found Johnson's shirt blacked about the bullit-hole, by the powder of the charge by which he was killed, whereupon they examined into the distance Smith stood from Johnson when he shot, and one of the assailants being admitted to oath, swore to the respective spots of ground they both stood on at that time, which the jury measured, and found to be twenty-three feet, nearly; then trying the experiment of shooting at the same shirt, both with and against the wind, and at the same distance, found no effects, not the least stain from the powder, on the shirt: –And let any person that pleases, make the experiment, and I will venture to affirm he shall find that powder will not stain at half the distance above mentioned, if shot out of a rifle gun, which Smith's was. Upon the whole, the jury, after the most accurate examination, and mature deliberation, brought in their verdict that some of the assailants themselves must necessarily have been the perpetrators of the murder.

"I have now represented the matter in its true and genuine colors, and which I will abide by. I only beg liberty to make a few remarks and reflections on the above mentioned extract. The author says "James Smith, with two others in company, passed round the town, without touching," by which it is plain he would insinuate, and make the public believe that Smith, and that part of the company, had taken some bye road, which is utterly false, for it was the king's high-way, and the straightest, that through Bedford, being something to the one side, nor would the other part of the company have gone through the town, but for the reason already given. Again, the author says that "four men were sent in pursuit of Smith and his companions, who over-took them about five miles from Bedford, and commanded them to surrender, on which Smith presented his gun at one of the men, who was struggling with his companion, fired it at him, and shot his companion through the back." Here I would just remark again, the unfair and partial account given of this matter, by the author; not a word mentioned of George's snapping his pistol before Smith offered to shoot, or of another of the assailants actually firing his pistol, though he confessed himself afterwards, he had done so; not the least mention of the company's baggage, which, to men in the least open to a fair inquiry, would have been sufficient proof of the innocence of their intentions. Must not an effusive blush overspread the face of the partial representer of facts, when he finds the veil he had thrown over truth thus pulled aside, and she exposed to naked view. Suppose it should be granted that Smith shot the man, (which is not, and I presume never can be proven to be the case) I would only ask, was he not on his own defence? Was he not publicly assaulted? Was he not charged at the peril of his life, to surrender, without knowing for what? No warrant being shown him, or any declaration made of their authority. And seeing these things are so, would any judicious man, any person in the least acquainted with the laws of the land, or morality, judge him guilty of wilful murder? But I humbly presume every one who has an opportunity of seeing this, will by this time be convinced that the proceedings against Smith were truly unlawful and tyranical, perhaps unparalleled by any instance in a civilized nation;

for to endeavor to kill a man in the apprehending him, in order to bring him to trial for a fact, and that too on a supposed one, is undoubtedly beyond all bounds of law or government.

"If the author of the extract thinks I have treated him unfair, or that I have advanced any thing he can controvert, let him come forward as a fair antagonist, and make his defence, and I will, if called upon, vindicate all that I have advanced against him or his abettors.

" WILLIAM SMITH. "

I remained in prison four months, and during this time I often thought of those that were confined in the time of the persecution, who declared their prison was converted into a palace. I now learned what this meant, as I never since, or before, experienced four months of equal happiness.

When the supreme court sat, I was severely prosecuted. At the commencement of my trial, the judges in a very unjust and arbitrary manner, rejected several of my evidences; yet, as Robert George (one of those who were in the fray when I was taken) swore in court that he snapped a pistol at me before I shot, and a concurrence of corroborating circumstances, amounted to strong presumptive evident that it could not possibly be my gun that killed Johnson, the jury, without hesitation, brought in their verdict, NOT GUILTY. One of the judges then declared that not one of this jury should ever hold any office above a constable. Notwithstanding this proud, ill-natured declaration, some of these jurymen afterwards filled honorable places, and I myself was elected the next year, and sat on the board * in Bedford county, and afterwards I served in the board three years in Westmoreland county.

In the year 1774, another Indian war commenced, though at this time the white people were the aggressors. The prospect of this terrified the frontier inhabitants, insomuch that the great part on the Ohio waters, either fled over the mountains, eastward, or collected into forts. As the state of Pennsylvania apprehended great danger, they at

---

* A board of commissioners was annually elected in Pennsylvania, to regulate taxes, and lay the county levy.

this time appointed me captain over what was then called the Pennsylvania line. As they knew I could raise men that would answer their purpose, they seemed to lay aside their former inveteracy.

In the year 1776, I was appointed a major in the Pennsylvania association. When American independence was declared, I was elected a member of the convention in Westmoreland county, state of Pennsylvania, and of the assembly as long as I proposed to serve.

While I attended the assembly in Philadelphia, in the year 1777, I saw in the street, some of my old boys, on their way to the Jerseys, against the British, and they desired me to go with them—I petitioned the house for leave of absence, in order to head a scouting party, which was granted me. We marched into the Jerseys, and went before General Washington's army, way-laid the road at Rocky Hill, attacked about two hundred of the British, and with thirty-six men drove them out of the woods into a large open field. After this we attacked a party that were guarding the officers baggage, and took the waggon and twenty-two Hessians; and also re-took some of our continental soldiers which they had with them. In a few days we killed and took more of the British, than was of our party. At this time, I took the camp fever, and was carried in a stage waggon to Burlington, where I lay until I recovered. When I took sick, my companion, Major James M'Common, took the command of the party, and had greater success than I had. If every officer and his party that lifted arms against the English, had fought with the same success that Major M'Common did, we would have made short work of the British war.

When I returned to Philadelphia, I applied to the assembly for leave to raise a battalion of riflemen, which they appeared very willing to grant, but said they could not do it, as the power of raising men and commissioning officers was at that time committed to General Washington, therefore they advised me to apply to his excellency. The following is a true copy of a letter of recommendation which I received at this time, from the council of safety:

" IN COUNCIL OF SAFETY,

" *Philadelphia, February 10th, 1777.*

" SIR,
" Application has been made to us by James Smith esq. of Westmoreland, a gentleman well acquainted with the Indian customs,

and their manners of carrying on war, for leave to raise a battallion of marks-men, expert in the use of rifles, and such as are acquainted with the Indian method of fighting, to be dressed entirely in their fashion, for the purpose of annoying and harrassing the enemy in their marches and encampments. We think two or three hundred men in that way, might be very useful. Should your excellency be of the same opinion, and direct such a corps to be formed, we will take proper measures for raising the men on the frontiers of this state, and follow such other directions as your excellency shall give in this matter.

" To his excellency General Washington. "

" The foregoing is a copy of a letter to his excellency General Washington, from the council of safety.

" JACOB S. HOWELL,
" Secretary. "

After this I received another letter of recommendation, which is as follows:

" We, whose names are under written, do certify that James Smith (now of the county of Westmoreland) was taken prisoner by the Indians, in an expedition before General Braddock's defeat, in the year 1755, and remained with them until the year 1760: and also that he served as ensign, in the year 1763, under the pay of the province of Pennsylvania, and as lieutenant, in the year 1764, and as captain, in the year 1774; and as a military officer he has sustained a good character. And we do recommend him as a person well acquainted with the Indian's method of fighting, and, in our humble opinion, exceedingly fit for the command of a ranging or scouting party, which we are also humbly of opinion, he could (if legally authorized) soon raise. Given under our hands at Philadelphia, this 13th day of March, 1777.

Thomas Paxton, capt.
William Duffield, esq.
David Robb, esq.
John Piper, col.
William M'Comb.
William Pepper, lieut. col.
James M'Clane, esq.

John Procter, col.
Jonathan Hoge, esq.
William Parker, capt.
Robert Elliot,
Joseph Armstrong, col.
Robert Peebles, lieut. col.
Samuel Patton, capt.
William Lyon, esq. "

With these, and some other letters of recommendation, which I have not now in my possession, I went to his excellency, who lay at Morristown. Though General Washington did not fall in with the scheme of white men turning Indians, yet he proposed giving me a major's place in a battallion of riflemen already raised. I thanked the general for his proposal; but as I entertained no high opinion of the colonel that I was to serve under, and with him I had no prospect of getting my old boys again, I thought I would be of more use in the cause we were then struggling to support, to remain with them as a militia officer, therefore I did not accept this offer.

In the year 1778, I received a colonel's commission, and after my return to Westmoreland, the Indians made an attack upon our frontiers. I then raised men and pursued them, and the second day we overtook and defeated them. We likewise took four scalps, and recovered the horses and plunder which they were carrying off. At the time of this attack, Captain John Hinkston pursued an Indian, both their guns being empty, and after the fray was over he was missing: – While we were enquiring about him, he came walking up, seemingly unconcerned, with a bloody scalp in his hand—he had pursued the Indian about a quarter of a mile, and tomahawked him.

Not long after this I was called upon to command four hundred riflemen, on an expedition against the Indian town on French Creek. It was some time in November before I received orders from General M'Intosh, to march, and then we were poorly equipped, and scarce of provisions. We marched in three columns, forty rod from each other. There were also flankers on the outside of each column, that marched a-breast in the rear, in scattered order—and even in the columns, the men were one rod apart—and in the front, the volunteers marched a-breast, in the same manner of the flankers, scouring the woods. In case of an attack, the officers were immediately to order the men to face out and take trees—in this position the Indians could not avail themselves by surrounding us, or have an opportunity of shooting a man from either side of the tree. If attacked, the center column was to reinforce what-ever part appeared to require it the most. When we encamped, our encampment formed a hollow square, including about thirty or forty acres—on the outside of the square there were centinels placed, whose business it was to watch for the enemy, and see that neither horses or bullocks went out: –And when encamped, if any attacks were made by an enemy, each officer was immediately to order the men to face out and take trees, as before mentioned; and in this form they could not take the advantage by surrounding us, as they commonly had done when they fought the whites.

The following is a copy of general orders, given at this time, which I have found among my journals:

" AT CAMP—OPPOSITE FORT PITT,

" *November 29th, 1778.*

" GENERAL ORDERS:
" *A copy thereof is to be given to each captain and subaltern, and to be read to each company.*

" You are to march in three columns, with flankers on the front and rear, and to keep a profound silence, and not to fire a gun, except at the enemy, without particular orders for that purpose; and in case of an attack, let it be so ordered that every other man only, is to shoot at once, excepting on extraordinary occasions. The one half of the men to keep a reserve fire, until their comrades load; and let every one be particularly careful not to fire at any time without a view of the enemy, and that not at too great a distance. I earnestly urge the above caution, as I have known very remarkable and grevious errors of this kind. You are to encamp on the hollow square, except the volunteers, who, according to their own request, are to encamp on the front of the square, a sufficient number of centinels are to be kept round the square at a proper distance. Every man is to be under arms at the break of day, and to parade opposite to their fire places, facing out, and when the officers examine their arms and find them in good order, and give necessary directions, they are to be dismissed, with orders to have their arms near them, and be always in readiness.
" Given by
" JAMES SMITH, *Colonel.* "

In this manner we proceeded on, to French Creek, where we found the Indian town evacuated. I then went on further than my orders called for, in quest of Indians; but our provisions being nearly exhausted, we were obliged to return. On our way back we met with considerable difficulties on account of high waters and scarcity of provision; yet we never lost one horse, excepting some that gave out.

After peace was made with the Indians, I met with some of them in Pittsburg, and enquired of them in their own tongue, concerning this expedition,—not letting them know I was there. They told me that they watched the movements of this army ever after they had left Fort-Pitt, and as they passed thro the glades or barrens they had a full view of them from the adjacent hills, and computed their number to be about one thousand. They said they also examined their camps, both before and after they were gone, and found, they could not make an advantageous attack, and therefore moved off from their town and hunting ground before we arrived.

In the year 1788 I settled in Bourbon county, Kentucky, seven miles above Paris; and in the same year was elected a member of the convention that sat at Danville, to confer about a separation from the state of Virginia; –and from that year until the year 1799, I represented Bourbon county, either in convention or as a member of the general assembly, except two years that I was left a few votes behind.

ON THE MANNERS AND CUSTOMS OF THE INDIANS.

The Indians are a slovenly people in their dress. –They seldom ever wash their shirts, and in regard to cookery they are exceeding filthy. When they kill a buffaloe they will sometimes lash the paunch of it round a sapling, and cast it into the kettle, boil it and sup the broth; tho they commonly shake it about in cold water, then boil and eat it. –Notwithstanding all this, they are very polite in their own way, and they retain among them, the essentials of good manners; tho they have few compliments, yet they are complaisant to one another, and when accompanied with good humor and discretion, they entertain strangers in the best manner their circumstances will admit. They use but few titles of honor. In the military line, the titles of great men are only captains or leaders of parties—In the civil line, the titles are only councilors, chiefs or the old wisemen. These titles are never made use of in addressing any of their great men. The language commonly made use of in addressing them, is, Grandfather, Father, or Uncle. They have no such thing in use among them, as Sir, Mr. Madam or Mistress—The common mode of address is, my Friend, Brother, Cousin, or Mother, Sister, &c. They pay great respect to age; or to the aged Fathers and Mothers among them of every rank. No one can arrive at any place of honor, among them, but by merit. Either some exploit in war, must be performed, before any one can be advanced in the military line, or become eminent for wisdom before they can obtain a seat in council. It would appear to the Indians a most ridiculous thing to see a man lead off a company of warriors, as an officer, who had himself never been in a battle in his life: even in case of merit, they are slow in advancing any one, until they arrive at or near middle-age.

They invite every one that comes to their house, or camp to eat, while they have any thing to give; and it is accounted bad manners to refuse eating, when invited. They are very tenacious of their old mode of dressing and painting, and do not change their fashions as we do. They are very fond of tobacco, and the men almost all smoke it mixed with sumach leaves or red willow bark, pulverized; tho they seldom use it any other way. They make use of the pipe also as a token of love and friendship.

In courtship they also differ from us. It is a common thing among them for a young woman, if in love, to make suit to a young man; tho the first address may be by the man; yet the other is the most common. The squaws are generally very immodest in their words and actions, and will often put the young men to the blush. The men commonly appear to be possessed of much more modesty than the women; yet I have been acquainted with some young squaws that appeared really modest: genuine it must be, as they were under very little restraint in the channel of education or custom.

When the Indians meet one another, instead of saying, how do you do, they commonly salute in the following manner—you are my friend—the reply is, truly friend, I am your friend—or, cousin, you yet exist—the reply is certainly I do. —They have their children under tolerable command: seldom ever whip them, and their common mode of chastising, is by ducking them in cold water; therefore their children are more obedient in the winter season, than they are in the summer; tho they are then not so often ducked. They are a peaceable people, and scarcely ever wrangle or scold, when sober; but they are very much addicted to drinking, and men and women will become basely intoxicated, if they can, by any means, procure or obtain spirituous liquor; and then they are commonly either extremely merry and kind, or very turbulent, ill-humored and disorderly.

ON THEIR TRADITIONS AND RELIGIOUS SENTIMENTS.

As the family that I was adopted into was intermarried with the Wiandots and Ottawas, three tongues were commonly spoke, viz. Caughnewaga, or what the French call Iroque, also the Wiandot and

Ottawa; by this means I had an opportunity of learning these three tongues; and I found that these nations varied in their traditions and opinions concerning religion; —and even numbers of the same nations differed widely in their religious sentiments. Their traditions are vague, whimsical, romantic and many of them scarce worth relating; and not any of them reach back to the creation of the world. The Wiandots comes the nearest to this. They tell of a squaw that was found when an infant, in the water in a canoe made of bull-rushes: this squaw became a great prophetess and did many wonderful things; she turned water into dry land, and at length made this continent, which was, at that time, only a very small island, and but a few Indians in it. Tho they were then but few they had not sufficient room to hunt; therefore this squaw went to the water side, and prayed that this little island might be enlarged. The great being then heard her prayer, and sent great numbers of Water Tortoises, and Muskrats, which brought with them mud and other materials, for enlarging this island, and by this means, they say, it was increased to the size that it now remains; therefore they say, that the white people ought not to encroach upon them, or take their land from them, because their great grand mother made it. —They say, that about this time the angels or heavenly inhabitants, as they call them, frequently visited them and talked with their forefathers; and gave directions how to pray, and how to appease the great being when he was offended. They told them that they were to offer sacrifice, burn tobacco, buffaloe and deer bones; but that they were not to burn bears or racoons bones in sacrifice.

The Ottawas say, that there are two great beings that rule and govern the universe, who are at war with each other; the one they call *Maneto*, and the other *Matchemaneto*. They say that Maneto is all kindness and love, and that Matchemaneto is an evil spirit, that delights in doing mischief; and some of them think, that they are equal in power, and therefore worship the evil spirit out of a principle of fear. Others doubt which of the two may be the most powerful, and therefore endeavor to keep in favor with both, by giving each of them some kind of worship. Others say that Maneto is the first great cause and therefore must be all-powerful and supreme, and ought to be adored and worshipped; whereas Matchemaneto ought to be rejected and dispised.

Those of the Ottawas that worship the evil spirit, pretend to be great conjurors. I think if there is any such thing now in the world as witchcraft, it is among these people. I have been told wonderful stories concerning their proceedings; but never was eye witness to any thing that appeared evidently supernatural.

Some of the Wiandots and Caughnewagas profess to be Roman-catholics; but even these retain many of the notions of their ancestors. Those of them who reject the Roman-catholic religion, hold that there is one great first cause, whom they call *Owaneeyo*, that rules and governs the universe, and takes care of all his creatures, rational and irrational, and gives them their food in due season, and hears the prayers of all those that call upon him; therefore it is but just and reasonable to pray, and offer sacrifice to this great being, and to do those things that are pleasing in his sight; —but they differ widely in what is pleasing or displeasing to this great being. Some hold that following nature or their own propensities is the way to happiness, and cannot be displeasing to the deity, because he delights in the happiness of his creatures, and does nothing in vain; but gave these dispositions with a design to lead to happiness, and therefore they ought to be followed. Others reject this opinion altogether, and say that following their own propensities in this manner, is neither the means of happiness nor the way to please the deity.

Tecaughretanego was of opinion that following nature in a limited sense was reasonable and right. He said that most of the irrational animals by following their natural propensities, were led to the greatest pitch of happiness that their natures and the world they live in would admit of. He said that mankind and the rattle snakes had evil dispositions, that led them to injure themselves and others. He gave instances of this. He said he had a puppy that he did not intend to raise, and in order to try an experiment, he tyed this puppy on a pole and held it to a rattle snake, which bit it several times; that he observed the snake shortly after, rolling about apparently in great misery, so that it appeared to have poisoned itself as well as the puppy. The other instance he gave was concerning himself. He said that when he was a young man, he was very fond of the women, and at length got the venereal disease, so that by following this propensity, he was led to injure himself and others. He said our happiness depends on our using our reason, in order to suppress these evil dispositions; but when our propensities neither lead us to injure ourselves nor others, we might with safety indulge them, or even pursue them as the means of happiness.

The Indians generally are of opinion that there are great numbers of inferior Deities, which they call *Carreyagaroona*, which signifies the Heavenly Inhabitants. These beings they suppose are employed as assistants, in managing the affairs of the universe, and in inspecting the actions of men: and that even the irrational animals are engaged in viewing their actions, and bearing intelligence to the Gods. The eagle, for this purpose, with her keen eye, is soaring about in the day, and the owl, with her nightly eye, perched on the trees around their camp in the night; therefore, when they observe the eagle or the owl near, they immediately offer sacrifice, or burn tobacco, that they may have a good report to carry to the Gods. They say that there are also great numbers of evil spirits, which they call *Onasahroona*, which signifies the Inhabitants of the Lower Region. These they say are employed in disturbing the world, and the good spirits are always going after them, and setting things right, so that they are constantly working in opposition to each other. Some talk of a future state, but not with any certainty: at best their notions are vague and unsettled. Others deny a future state altogether, and say that after death they neither think or live.

As the Caughnewagas and the six nations speak nearly the same language, their theology is also nearly alike. When I met with the Shawanees or Delawares, as I could not speak their tongue, I spoke Ottawa to them, and as it bore some resemblance to their language, we understood each other in some common affairs, but as I could only converse with them very imperfectly, I cannot from my own knowledge, with certainty, give any account of their theological opinions.

ON THEIR POLICE OR CIVIL GOVERNMENT

I have often heard of Indian Kings, but never saw any. —How any term used by the Indians in their own tongue, for the chief man of a nation, could be rendered King, I know not. The chief of a nation is neither a supreme ruler, monarch or potentate—He can neither make war or peace, leagues or treaties—He cannot impress soldiers, or dispose of magazines—He cannot adjourn, prorogue or dissolve a general assembly, nor can he refuse his assent to their conclusions, or in any manner controul them—With them there is no such thing as hereditary succession, title of nobility or royal blood, even talked of—The chief of a nation, even with the consent of his assembly, or council, cannot raise one shilling of tax off the citizens, but only receive what they please to give as free and voluntary donations. —The chief of a nation has to hunt for his living, as any other citizen—How then can they with any propriety, be called kings? I apprehend that the white people were formerly so fond of the name of kings, and so ignorant of their power, that they concluded the chief man of a nation must be a king.

As they are illiterate, they consequently have no written code of laws. What they execute as laws, are either old customs, or the immediate result of new councils. Some of their ancient laws or customs are very pernicious, and disturb the public weal. Their vague law of marriage is a glaring instance of this, as the man and his wife are under no legal obligation to live together, if they are both willing to part. They have little form, or ceremony among them, in matrimony, but do like the Israelites of old—the man goes in unto the woman, and she becomes his wife. The years of puberty and the age of consent, is about fourteen for the women, and eighteen for the men. Before I was taken by the Indians, I had often heard that in the ceremony of marriage, the man gave the woman a deer's leg, and she gave him a red ear of corn, signifying that she was to keep him in bread, and he was to keep her in meat. I enquired of them concerning the truth of this, and they said they knew nothing of it, further than they had heard that it was the ancient custom among some nations. Their frequent changing of partners prevents propagation, creates disturbances, and often occasions murder and bloodshed; though this is commonly committed under pretense of being drunk. Their impunity to crimes committed when intoxicated with spirituous liquors, or their admitting one crime as an excuse for another, is a very unjust law or custom.

The extremes they run into in dividing the necessaries of life, are hurtful to the public weal; though their dividing meat when hunting, may answer a valuable purpose, as one family may have success one day, and the other the next; but their carrying this custom to the town, or to agriculture, is striking at the root of industry, as industrious persons ought to be rewarded, and the lazy suffer for their indolence.

They have scarcely any penal laws: the principal punishment is degrading: even murder is not punished by any formal law, only the friends of the murdered are at liberty to slay the murderer, if some atonement is not made. Their not annexing penalties to their laws, is perhaps not as great a crime, or as unjust and cruel, as the bloody penal laws of England, which we have so long shamefully practiced, and which are in force in this state, until our penitentiary house is finished, which is now building, and then they are to be repealed.

Let us also take a view of the advantages attending Indian police: —They are not oppressed or perplexed with expensive litigation— They are not injured by legal robbery—They have no splendid villains that make themselves grand and great on other people's labor—They have neither church or state erected as money-making machines.

ON THEIR DISCIPLINE, AND METHOD OF WAR.

I have often heard the British officers call the Indians the undisciplined savages, which is a capital mistake—as they have all the essentials of discipline. They are under good command, and punctual in obeying orders: they can act in concert, and when their officers lay a plan and give orders, they will cheerfully unite in putting all their directions into immediate execution; and by each man observing the motion or movement of his right hand companion, they can communicate the motion from right to left, and march abreast in concert, and in scattered order, though the line may be more than a mile long, and continue, if occasion requires, for a considerable distance, without disorder or confusion. They can perform various necessary maneuvers, either slowly, or as fast as they can run: they can form a circle, or semi-circle: the circle they make use of, in order to surround their enemy, and the semi-circle if the enemy has a river on one side of them. They can also form a large hollow square, face out and take trees: this they do, if their enemies are about surrounding them, to prevent from being shot from either side of the tree. When they go into battle they are not loaded or encumbered with many clothes, as they commonly fight naked, save only breech-clout, leggins and mockesons. There is no such thing as corporeal punishment used, in order to bring them under such good discipline: degrading is the only chastisement, and they are so unanimous in this, that it effectually answers the purpose. Their officers plan, order and conduct matters until they are brought into action, and then each man is to fight as though he was to gain the battle himself. General orders are commonly given in time of battle, either to advance or retreat, and is done by a shout or yell, which is well understood, and then they retreat or advance in concert. They are generally well equipped, and exceeding expert and active in the use of arms. Could it be supposed that undisciplined troops could defeat Generals Braddock, Grant, &c? It may be said by some that the French were also engaged in this war: true, they were; yet I know it was the Indians that laid the plan, and with small assistance, put it into execution. The Indians had no aid from the French, or any other power, when they besieged Fort Pitt in the year 1763, and cut off the communication for a considerable time, between that post and Fort Loudon, and would have defeated General Bouquet's army, (who were on the way to raise the siege) had it not been for assistance of the Virginia volunteers. They had no British troops with them when they defeated Colonel Crawford, near the Sandusky, in the time of the American War with Great Britain; or when they defeated Colonel Loughrie, on the Ohio, near the Miami, on his way to meet General Clarke: this was also in the time of the British war. It was the Indians alone that defeated Colonel Todd, in Kentucky, near the Blue licks, in the year 1782; and Colonel Harmer, betwixt the Ohio and Lake Erie, in the year 1790, and General St. Clair, in the year 1791; and it is said that there was more of our men killed at this defeat, than there were in any one battle during our contest with Great Britain. They had no aid when they fought even the Virginia rifle-men almost a whole day, at the Great Kanhawa, in the year 1774; and when they found they could not prevail against the Virginians, they made a most artful retreat. Notwithstanding they had the Ohio to cross, some continued firing, whilst others were crossing the river; in this manner they proceeded until they all got over, before the Virginians knew that they had retreated; and in this retreat they carried off all their wounded. In the most of the foregoing defeats, they fought with an inferior number, though in this, I believe it was not the case.

Nothing can be more unjustly represented than the different accounts we have had of their number from time to time, both by their own computations, and that of the British. While I was among them, I saw the account of the number, that they in those parts gave to the French, and kept it by me. When they in their own council-house, were taking an account of their number, with a piece of bark newly stripped, and a small stick, which answered the end of a slate and pencil, I took an account of the different nations and tribes, which I added together, and found there were not half the number which they had given the French; and though they were then their allies, and lived among them, it was not easy finding out the deception, as they were a wandering set, and some of them almost always in the woods hunting. I asked one of the chiefs what was their reason for making such different returns? He said it was for political reasons, in order to obtain great presents from the French, by telling them they could not divide such and such quantities of goods among so many.

In year of General Bouquet's last campaign, 1764, I saw the official return made by the British officers, of the number of Indians that were in arms against us that year, which amounted to thirty thousand. As I was then a lieutenant in the British service, I told them I was of opinion that there was not above one thousand in arms against us, as they were divided by Broadstreet's army being then at Lake Erie. The British officers hooted at me, and said they could not make England sensible of the difficulties they labored under in fighting them, as England expects that their troops could fight the undisciplined savages in America, five to one, as they did the East-Indians, and therefore my report would not answer their purpose, as they could not give an honorable account of the war, but by augmenting their number. I am of opinion that from Braddock's war, until the present time, there never were more than three thousand Indians at any time, in arms against us, west of Fort Pitt, and frequently not half that number. According to the Indians' own accounts during the whole of Braddock's war, or from 1755, till 1758, they killed or took, fifty of our people, for one that they lost. In the war that commenced in the year 1763, they killed, comparatively, few of our people, and lost more of theirs, as the frontiers (especially the Virginians) had learned something of their method of war: yet, they, in this war, according to their own accounts, (which I believe to be true) killed or took ten of our people, for one they lost.

Let us now take a view of the blood and treasure that was spent in opposing comparatively, a few Indian warriors, with only some assistance from the French, the first four years of the war. Additional to the amazing destruction and slaughter that the frontiers sustained, from James River to Susquehanna, and about thirty miles broad; the following campaigns were also carried on against the Indians: — General Braddock's, in the year 1755: Colonel Armstrong's against the Cattanyan town, on the Alleghany, 1757: General Forbes', in 1758: General Stanwick's, in 1759: General Monkton's, in 1760: Colonel Bouquet's, 1761—and 1763, when he fought the battle of Bushy Run, and lost above one hundred men; but by the assistance of the Virginia volunteers, drove the Indians: Colonel Armstrong's, up the West Branch of Susquehanna, in 1763: General Broadstreet's, up Lake Erie, in 1764: General Bouquet's, against the Indians at Muskingum, in 1764: Lord Dunmore's, in 1774: General M'Intosh's, in 1778: Colonel Crawford's, shortly after his, General Clarke's in 1778—1780: Colonel

Bowman's, 1779: General Clarke's in 1782—against the Wabash, in 1786: General Logan's against the Shawanees in 1786: General Wilkinson's in _____: Colonel Harmer's in 1790: and General St. Clair's, in 1791; which, in all, are twenty-two campaigns, besides smaller expeditions, such as the French Creek expedition, Colonels Edward's, Loughrie's, &c. All these were exclusive of the number of men that were internally employed as scouting parties, and in erecting forts, guarding stations, &c. When we take the foregoing occurrences into consideration, may we not reasonably conclude, that they are the best disciplined troops in the known world? Is it not the best discipline that has the greatest tendency to annoy the enemy and save their own men? I apprehend that the Indian discipline is as well calculated to answer the purpose in the woods of America, as the British discipline in Flanders: and British discipline in the woods, is the way to have men slaughtered, with scarcely any chance of defending themselves.

Let us take a view of the benefits we have received, by what little we have learned of their art of war, which cost us dear, and the loss that we have sustained for want of it, and then see if it will not be well worth our while to retain what we have, and also to endeavor to improve in this necessary branch of business. Though we have made considerable proficiency in this line, and in some respects out-do them, *viz.* as marksmen, and in cutting our rifles, and in keeping them in good order; yet, I apprehend we are far behind in their manoeuvres, or in being able to surprize, or prevent a surprize. May we not conclude that the progress we had made in their art of war, contributed considerably towards our success, in various respects, when contending with great Britain for liberty? Had the British king, attempted to enslave us before Braddock's war, in all probability he might readily have done it, because, except the New-Englanders, who had formerly been engaged in war, with the Indians, we were unacquainted with any kind of war: but after fighting such a subtil and barbarous enemy as the Indians, we were not terrified at the approach of British red-coats. —Was not Burgoyne's defeat accomplished in some measure by the Indian mode of fighting? and did not Gen. Morgan's rifle-men, and many others, fight with greater success, in consequence of what they had learned of their art of war? Kentucky would not have been settled at the time it was, had the Virginians been altogether ignorant of this method of war.

In Braddock's war, the frontiers were laid waste, for above three hundred miles long, and generally about thirty broad, excepting some that were living in forts, and many hundreds, or perhaps thousands, killed or made captives, and horses, and all kinds of property carried off: but, in the next Indian war, though we had the same Indians to cope with, the frontiers almost all stood their ground, because they were by this time, in some measure acquainted with their manoeuvres; and the want of this, in the first war, was the cause of the loss of many hundreds of our citizens, and much treasure.

Though large volumes have been wrote on morality, yet it may all be summed up in saying, do as you would wish to be done by: so the Indians sum up the art of war in the following manner:

The business of the private warriors is to be under command, or punctually to obey orders—to learn to march a-breast in scattered order, so as to be in readiness to surround the enemy, or to prevent being surrounded—to be good marksmen, and active in the use of arms—to practice running—to learn to endure hunger or hardships with patience and fortitude—to tell the truth at all times to their officers, but more especially when sent out to spy the enemy.

Concerning Officers. They say that it would be absurd to appoint a man an officer whose skill and courage had never been tried—that all officers should be advanced only according to merit—that no one man should have the absolute command of an army—that a council of officers are to determine when, and how an attack is to be made—that it is the business of the officers to lay plans to take every advantage of the enemy—to ambush and surprize them, and to prevent being ambushed and suprized themselves—it is the duty of officers to prepare and deliver speeches to the men, in order to annimate and encourage them; and on the march, to prevent the men, at any time, from getting into a huddle, because if the enemy should surround them in this position, they would be exposed to the enemy's fire. It is likewise their business at all times to endeavor to annoy their enemy, and save their own men, and therefore ought never to bring on an attack without considerable advantage, or without what appeared to them the sure prospect of victory, and that with the loss of few men: and if at any time they should be mistaken in this, and are like to lose many men by gaining the victory, it is their duty to retreat, and wait for a better opportunity of defeating their enemy, without the danger of losing so many men. Their conduct proves that they act upon these principles, therefore it is, that from Braddock's war to the present time, they have seldom ever made an unsuccessful attack. The battle at the mouth of the Great Kanhawa, is the greatest instance of this; and even then, though the Indians killed about three, for one they lost, yet they retreated. The loss of the Virginians in this action, was seventy killed and the same number wounded: —The Indians lost twenty killed on the field, and eight, who died afterwards, of their wounds. This was the greatest loss of men that I ever knew the Indians to sustain in any one battle. They will commonly retreat if their men are falling fast— they will not stand cutting, like the Highlanders, or other British troops: but this proceeds from a compliance with their rules of war, rather than cowardice. If they are surrounded, they will fight while there is a man of them alive, rather than surrender. When Colonel John Armstrong surrounded the Cattanyan town, on the Allegheny river, Captain Jacobs, a Delaware chief, with some warriors, took possession of a house, defended themselves for some time, and killed a number of our men. As Jacobs could speak English, our people called on him to surrender: he said that he and his men were warriors, and they would all fight while life remained. He was again told that they should be well used, if they would only surrender; and if not, the house should be burned down over their heads: —Jacobs replied he could eat fire: and when the house was in a flame, he, and they that were with him, came out in a fighting position, and were all killed. As they are a sharp, active kind of people, and war is their principal study, in this they have arrived at considerable perfection. We may learn of the Indians what is useful and laudable, and at the same time lay aside their barbarous proceedings. It is much to be lamented that some of our frontier rifle-men are prone to imitate them in their inhumanity. During the British war, a considerable number of men from below Fort Pitt, crossed the Ohio, and marched into a town of Friendly Indians, chiefly Delawares, who professed the Moravian religion. As the Indians apprehended no danger, they neither lifted arms or fled. After these rifle-men were sometime in the town, and the Indians altogether in their power, in cool blood, they massacred the whole town, without distinction of age or sex. This was an act of barbarity beyond any thing I ever knew to be committed by the savages themselves.

Why have we not made greater proficiency in the Indian art of war? Is it because we are too proud to imitate them, even though it should be a means of preserving the lives of many of our citizens? No! We are not above borrowing language from them, such as homony, pone, tomahawk, &c. which is little or no use to us. I apprehend that the reasons why we have not improved more in this respect, are as follows: no important acquisition is to be obtained but by attention and diligence; and as it is easier to learn to move and act in concert, in close order, in the open plain, than to act in concert in scattered order, in the woods; so it is easier to learn our discipline, than the Indian manoeuvres. They train up their boys to the art of war from the time they are twelve or fourteen years of age; whereas the principal chance our people had of learning, was by observing their movements when in action against us. I have been long astonished that no one has wrote upon this important subject, as their art of war would not only be of use to us in case of another rupture with them; but were only part of our men taught this art, accompanied with our continental discipline, I think no European power, after trial, would venture to shew its head in the American woods.

If what I have wrote should meet the approbation of my countrymen, perhaps I may publish more upon this subject, in a future edition.

E N D.

Made in the USA
Columbia, SC
14 March 2020